COUNTRY THREADS
Garner, Iowa USA

MARY TENDALL AND CONNIE TESENE

Country Threads©
© 1992 by Connie Tesene and Mary Tendall

That Patchwork Place, Inc.,
PO Box 118, Bothell, WA 98041-0118

Printed in the United States of America
97 96 95 94 93 92   6 5 4 3 2 1

Library of Congress Cataloging-in-Publication Data

Tesene, Connie
    Country threads / Connie Tesene and Mary Tendall.
        p.   cm. — (Quilt shop series)
    ISBN 1-56477-007-9
    1. Patchwork—Patterns. 2. Patchwork Quilts. I. Tendall, Mary,
II. Title   III. Series
TT835.T375   1992
746.46—dc20   91-47908
                                                            CIP

Published in the USA

Acknowledgments

Our special thanks go to:

Our families and staff who pitched in and helped free up our time so that we could sew and write this book.

Gladys Jurgemeyer who quilted every small quilt in this book and used her imagination on how to quilt them instead of asking us.

Vola Jass and Marie Thill for their fine quilting.

Ray Hanson for putting up with our pets during the photography sessions.

Carolyn Pope for proofreading and sewing with us until 3 a.m.

Pamela Lage for her excellent computer services.

Elnora M. Paulson for her wonderful "ziggle" machine quilting.

Credits

Photography . . . . Doug Plager
Illustration and Graphics . . . . Laurel Strand
                                                            Barb Tourtillotte
                                                            Susan Oldham
Text and Cover Design . . . . Judy Petry
Editor . . . . Barbara Weiland
Copy Editor . . . . Jane Meyer

CONTENTS

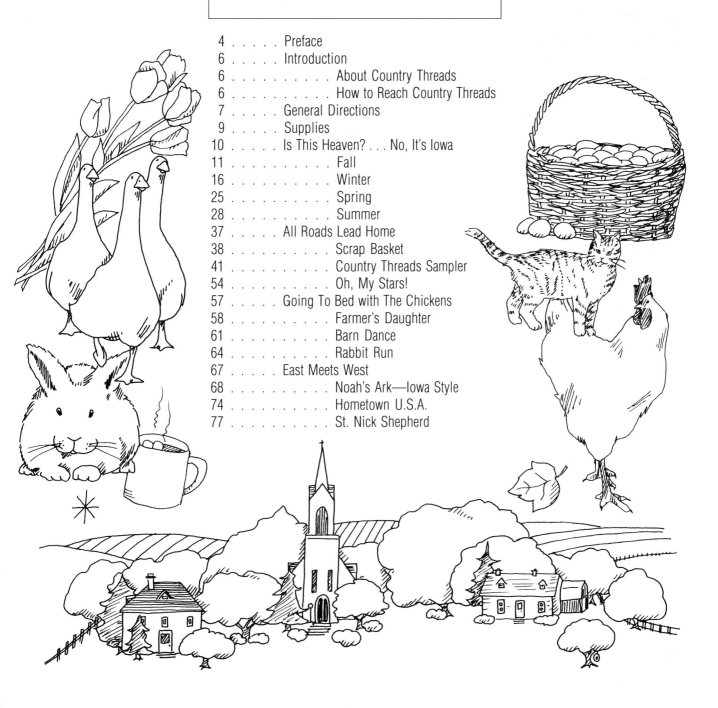

When asked to do this book, we took a deep breath and said, "Yes, we'd love to!" knowing we'd have not even three full months to complete it. Being aware of this condition before we agreed to do it, we learned that nothing is impossible and that it's sometimes fun to do something totally and completely consuming as long as you can see the end coming.

Being Iowa natives, we have grown up and lived the country life all our lives but it has never been more prominent than in our everyday working lives. The day begins early at Country Threads, with Mary and her husband, Russ, doing chores for the sheep, chickens, ducks, geese, goats, and cats. They all need to be fed and watered every morning and afternoon, 365 days a year.

The wild birds get preferential

PREFACE

treatment, too, as do the squirrels. In the winter, pheasants and white-tailed deer are also fed and watered if they're brave enough to come into the feeding area. In the spring, summer, and fall, the chickens roam freely on the farm, many times keeping the customers company as they walk down the lane to the quilt shop.

Jimmy, the angora goat, and Louise, the African pygmy goat, spend the warm days in a large pen beside the lane, visiting and begging leaves from the customers and their children who visit the shop.

Emma, the cat in residence, lives in the quilt shop year-round, sometimes not venturing outside for days, especially in the cold winter months. One of the daily chores for the staff is brushing Emma so that the fabric

COUNTRY THREADS

isn't covered with cat hair. Emma loves the attention and always wants to lie right on the quilt that has been laid out on the table for display, never the one in the back room out of sight.

Sally, the beloved golden Labrador, is no longer at the farm. She lived a privileged life for twelve and a half years that ended on August 12, 1991. We all miss her, as do many of our customers who were accustomed to being asked to "just step over the dog" when they came in the door.

The sheep, Twinkletoes, Munchkin, Mike, and Freckles, are all about twelve to fifteen years old. They will be allowed to live out their lives here at Country Threads and all they have to do is give up their wool every spring. After the wool is sheared in April or May, it is sent to a woolen mill to be washed and carded. It comes back to us in sheets and is then packaged in clear bags with a card telling which sheep's wool it was. Rose, a favorite sheep, died in August 1990. (Many of our customers have continued to request Rose's wool after receiving it in their orders.) Rose loved whole wheat bread, and since most of her teeth were missing for about a year before she died, she got bread in the morning instead of corn like the others. We have no idea how long the other sheep will be alive, but they will never be sold.

If you visit Country Threads—and we hope you do—please watch out for pets in the driveway and yard. The chickens usually wander by, the eleven cats are always willing to stop and "visit," and someday Russ and Mary will give another homeless dog a good home. If the day comes that the shop closes, it will immediately become a shelter for homeless pets—those older animals who are no longer wanted for one reason or another.

Being animal lovers affects our business atmosphere in many ways. The country life is a natural for us, and through the projects in this book, we've portrayed it in fabric.

Connie and Mary

INTRODUCTION

About Country Threads

Connie Tesene and Mary Tendall have been partners in Country Threads for ten years. The first seven years were spent operating a wholesale quilt pattern business out of a chicken coop on Mary's farm. In 1987 when the chicken house became too small, the Tendalls built a double garage with a large room upstairs, which became Country Threads' classroom. The following year, Connie and Mary purchased a used semitrailer and parked it next to the chicken coop for an unheated warehouse. In 1989 they expanded their business to include a retail quilt shop.

For the first few years, both Connie and Mary sewed full-time in their homes—Mary in her dining room and Connie in a little cubbyhole under the stairs. When business outgrew the space, each added a sewing room to her home, welcome additions for both families.

Today, Country Threads sends its original quilt patterns to quilt shops in every state and several foreign countries. The partners are the creators of more than 100 quilt patterns, a line of gift stationery and cards, and their most recent book, *On Behalf of Chickens.*

Connie and her husband, Roy, have three boys: Andy, 13; Joe, 11; and Dan, 9; as well as four cats—Megan, Rambo, Blackie, and Gilda. Roy, a dentist in Garner, has his office in a log cabin. The family enjoys boating in the summer and skiing in the winter. The boys are busy with musical instruments, sports, and many school, church, and scout activities. All are well versed in quilt names and patterns and often lend Connie their ideas for new quilt designs.

Mary and her husband, Russ, have many pets to care for as well as a small farm. Russ is a long-distance truck driver and travels in the Midwest and eastern states hauling freight. He enjoys playing duplicate bridge and gardening. Mary plays piano at her church and enjoys sports of all kinds. Her favorite is girls' high school basketball.

How to Reach Country Threads Quilt Shop

Garner, Iowa, is located in north central Iowa, due west of Mason City and about 100 miles due north of Des Moines.

To get to Country Threads traveling from the north or south on I-35, take the exit for Hwy. 18 West at Clear Lake, Iowa. Drive west on Hwy. 18 eleven miles to Garner. Three miles from the western edge of Garner, turn south off Hwy. 18 onto the gravel road. Country Threads is the first place on the right side of the road. There are road signs* from either direction on Hwy 18. and also at the driveway.

If you're traveling from the west, drive seven miles east of Britt on Hwy. 18, turn south on the gravel road, then turn right into the driveway.

Coming from the north from Forest City, the home of Winnebago motor homes, take Hwy. 69 south to the junction with Hwy. 18. Turn right (west) and travel two miles west on Hwy. 18. Watch for the road sign.

Coming from the south, take Hwy. 69 to the junction with Hwy. 18 at the west edge of Garner. Turn left and drive west three miles. Watch for the road sign.

* Road signs are regulation blue Department of Transportation signs.

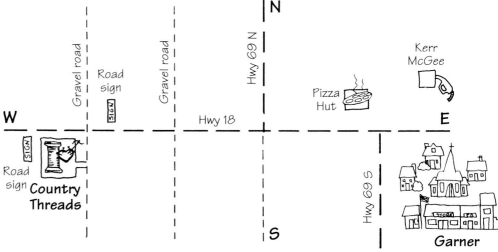

Read through all directions before beginning your project to make sure you have all the necessary supplies on hand. It will also be helpful to become familiar with the construction directions before you begin.

Templates

When full-size templates are given for a block, ¼" seam allowances have been included. If a block requires templates, rotary measurements have not been included. If the directions indicate that the pattern pieces can be cut with your rotary cutter, then all the pieces will be rotary cut. Rotary measurements include ¼"-wide seam allowances. Stitch with all pieces right sides together unless otherwise noted.

GENERAL DIRECTIONS

Borders

All borders in this book are cut as straight borders. The top and bottom are sewn on first, folded out, and pressed. Then the sides are added, folded out, and pressed. No mitered borders were used in any of the projects in this book.

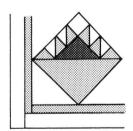

Binding

All wall quilts are bound with straight-cut strips, 1½" wide. Binding strips are added in the same order as the borders. Sew the top and bottom on first, trimming ends even with the quilt edges, fold out strip, and press. Then add the side binding strips. We prefer not to trim the batting and backing before sewing on the binding strips, as we find we can keep the binding stitching much straighter that way. After sewing the top and bottom binding strips to the quilt, trim away the excess batting and backing at the top and bottom edges. Fold out the top and bottom binding strips; press and add the side binding strips, trimming away the excess batting and backing at each side. Fold binding strips to the back of the quilt, turn under ¼" and slipstitch to the back of the quilt.

When binding a large, bed-size quilt, we cut continuous bias and double it when stitching it to the quilt.

Appliqué

Trace appliqué patterns onto the right side of the fabric and cut ⅛" to ¼" beyond the drawn line. Turn under the raw edge along the drawn line and baste by hand or press. Position the appliqué and, with matching thread, slipstitch it to the foundation piece. Remove basting stitches and press.

Cut

Baste

Slipstitch

Our staff handles the day-to-day retail and wholesale operations. Seated from left to right are Hazel Larson and Becky Rose. Standing from left to right are Roxanne Lamb, Carol Barker and Emma (the cat), Sue Urich and Laura Boehnke. We couldn't do it without them!

Connector Squares

In our quilt designs, we often use connector squares as an easy way of adding triangle corners onto rectangles or larger squares. This is especially true if the desired finished triangle is very small.

1. Place the connector square against the background piece, right sides together, in the desired corner (unless directed otherwise in the quilt directions).

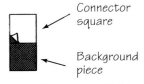

Connector square

Background piece

2. Stitch diagonally across the square, stitching from corner to corner.

3. Trim away the outside corner of the connector square. *Do not cut off the corner of the background block.* Fold corner square back over seam and press.

Overdyeing Fabrics

To achieve the warm, mellow antique look in our quilts, we often overdye the fabrics before cutting out the quilt. To do this you will need a tan-colored commercial dye. Follow the manufacturer's directions:

1. Fill your automatic washer with hot water. Dissolve the tan dye in a separate bowl and then add it to the hot water in the washing machine.
2. Wet fabrics first and put them into the washer filled with tan dye. Let the fabric soak until desired color is reached. Fabric is always darker when wet so leave it in until one shade darker than you want. It *will* dry lighter.
3. Remove fabric from hot water and hang on clothesline to drip dry, or wring out by hand and put in the dryer. Since you don't let the washer go through the entire wash cycle, you may wish to add more fabric to the dye water.
4. After fabric is dry, press (or leave wrinkles in, if desired).
5. Follow the manufacturer's directions to clean the washing machine. Also, don't forget to clean your dryer or your next white towels might be beige!!

Constructing Log Cabin Blocks

We use Log Cabin blocks in many of our quilts. Following are general instructions for Log Cabin construction.

1. Cut an assortment of light (#1) and dark (#2) strips for the logs, making them the desired finished width, plus ½" for seam allowances. Cut the center square the same size as the log width. For example, if you cut the strips 1½" wide, cut a 1½" x 1½" square for the center.
2. Place strip #1 on the center square, right sides together. Stitch a ¼"-wide seam. Trim strip even with bottom edge of center square. Fold out and press.

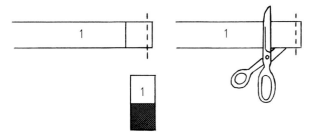

3. Turn so that strip #1 is at the "top." Place a second strip #1 along the right hand edge, right sides together. Stitch, trim, fold out, and press as shown in step 2.

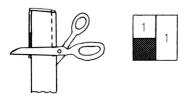

4. Place strip #2 along right hand edge, right sides together. Stitch, trim, fold out, and press. Turn block so #2 is at the "top." Stitch the next strip #2 to the right-hand side as shown in previous steps. Trim, fold out, and press.

5. Continue adding strips, *always* positioning the last strip you added at the "top" and *always* sewing the next strip along the right-hand side of the block.

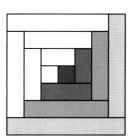

Fabric Selection

To get that "Country Threads look," we use a wide variety of fabrics, mixing many hues and intensities of a color together. We use mostly homespuns, stripes, plaids, checks, and small overall background designs. We rarely use large florals and seldom use multicolor florals in our quilts.

When the directions call for an assortment of red fabrics, for example, we pick fabrics that are rose, burgundy, true red, red-orange, and maroon and use them all together in the various blocks. When an assortment of light fabrics is required, we use scraps with backgrounds ranging in color from ivory to dark tan. Choose from homespuns, prints, checks, and solid-colored fabrics. Study the quilt photos carefully when choosing these fabrics. The idea is to use different shades of the color scheme in your quilt project to get the "look."

When figuring yardage, we try to estimate as closely as possible, but when using scraps, bits, and pieces, it is sometimes difficult to pinpoint the exact amount of fabric needed. If a large piece is needed in the quilt, that size will be noted in the materials list. Otherwise, we consider an assortment to total 3 yards—a combination of scraps, ⅛-yard pieces, fat quarters, and leftover pieces from previous projects. When working with scraps, you never need to worry about running out of any particular fabric since it was never meant to be "matched" in the first place. This is a very easygoing, laid-back way of picking fabrics, which works for us and creates the "look" we like.

We seldom cut plaids and checks on the straight of grain. By cutting across the width of the folded fabric and not paying attention to the grain line, we think we achieve a very homespun, old-time appearance in our quilts. Many of our students just can't get used to seeing plaids waver and wiggle across their quilts and to them we say, "If it bothers you, go ahead and cut the pieces on grain." After all, it's their quilt and we want them to be happy with the result. Likewise, we encourage you to cut plaids and checks the way that is most comfortable for you.

Batting

For all wall quilts, we use a low-loft, dense fleece that is sold by the yard from the bolt. It is usually 45" wide. We like our wall quilts to lay very flat when hung and this type of fleece gives us that look. For bed-size quilts, purchase the batt of your choice. Pieces of the 45"-wide fleece may even be whipstitched together to make the correct size for larger projects. Each project in this book calls for batting to finish, but leaves the specific type up to you.

Scissors

Use good-quality, sharp scissors to cut fabric and an older pair for cutting paper and cardboard. Use embroidery scissors to cut small appliqué pieces.

SUPPLIES

Rotary Equipment

Our favorite pieces of rotary equipment include a 6" x 12" clear acrylic ruler, a 24" x 36" gridded board, and a large rotary cutter. How did we ever make quilts without them? We also use a 24" acrylic ruler, and acrylic squares in 12", 6", and 4" sizes.

Sewing Machine

A good straight stitch is essential when making quilts. You do not need decorative stitches or a fancy machine, just one that's reliable so that you don't spend sewing time screaming at your machine!

Thread

We sew nearly everything with off-white thread unless we're sewing on black or navy. We never match colored thread as it's just too much bother.

Additional Supplies

Depending on the individual project, you may need some of the following supplies:

quilting thread
buttonhole twist
embroidery floss
hand quilting needles
seam ripper (oh no!)
marking pencils and tools
pins
iron
ironing board or pressing pad
polyester fiberfill
hot glue gun
permanent marker

IS THIS HEAVEN? . . . NO, IT'S IOWA!

❤ We love quilts done in seasonal themes and so do our customers. The four wall quilts in this group of designs represent our interpretation of each of the four seasons in Iowa. We think you'll agree that they evoke the following signs of the seasons:

Fall
Hayrides, burning leaves, caramel apples, school buses, pumpkins, Indian corn, Halloween, hot apple cider, and storm windows.

Winter
Dazzling, white snowdrifts, sub-zero temperatures, the smell of wood burning in the fireplace, snowplows, jumper cables, cross-country skis, snowmobiles, fresh pine boughs, and hot chocolate.

Spring
Budding trees, apple blossoms, green grass, baby animals, newly planted cornfields and gardens, fresh asparagus and rhubarb, roller skates, and lawn mowers.

Summer
The smell of grass and silking corn, hot, hazy days, buttered sweet corn, ripe tomatoes, weeds, garden flowers, baled hay, and the county fair.

❤ The invigorating weather that autumn brings helps make this one of the busiest and most beautiful seasons in Iowa. The fields of corn and beans that surround our homes are quickly harvested by efficient farmers who work long, hard hours to feed our hungry world. We all have a little farmer in us as we gather our garden vegetables, apples, and pumpkins to store for the long winter ahead.

FALL

Taking quiet walks in the woods, drinking steaming cups of hot cider, throwing an extra quilt on the bed, raking leaves, and roasting marshmallows over a bonfire are but a few fall activities for which we give thanks.

Finished Size: 24" x 37"

Is This Heaven? . . . No, It's Iowa in Fall by Country Threads, 1991, Garner, Iowa, 24" x 37". Pumpkins, turkeys, and maple leaves are combined with Log Cabin apples in a seasonal wall quilt. Quilted by Gladys Jurgemeyer.

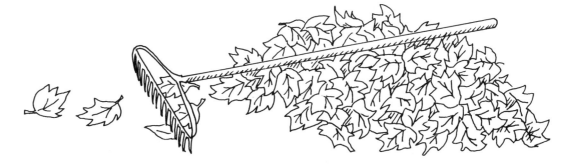

Materials

44"-wide fabric

¾ yd. assorted light fabrics
⅓ yd. assorted reds
⅓ yd. assorted oranges
⅓ yd. assorted browns
⅛ yd. assorted golds
⅛ yd. assorted blacks
⅛ yd. assorted greens
⅛ yd. assorted teals

⅛ yd. assorted pinks
⅛ yd. purple for inner border
¼ yd. green for outer border
⅝ yd. backing
Black embroidery floss
Batting, binding, and thread to finish

Directions

1. Cut and appliqué one Pumpkin block, using appliqué templates #1–#4 on pullout pattern insert. See page 7 for appliqué instructions.

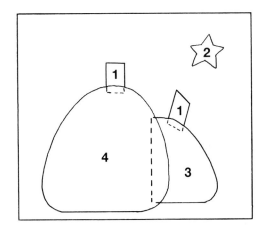

Pumpkin guide block
Make 1
Finished size: 10" x 12"

Cut 1 foundation block, 10½" x 12½", from a light fabric. Appliqué pieces #1–#4, referring to the guide block for positioning.

2. Rotary cut the following blocks. Templates are not required. Study each guide block to identify the various pattern pieces, which are all labeled by number.

Maple Leaf

Cut and piece 6 Maple Leaf blocks, with each leaf made from a different color on a different background. Cutting directions are for 1 block, using pieces #1 and #2. Read all directions before piecing the blocks.

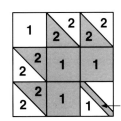

Maple Leaf guide block
Make 6
Finished size: 3" x 3"

Bias strip
Cut 3/4"

MAPLE LEAF BLOCKS (ROTARY-CUT)

Piece	Color	Cutting
#1	leaf color	3 squares, 1½" x 1½"
	light	2 squares, 1½" x 1½"
#2	leaf color	2 squares, 1⅞" x 1⅞"
		Cut once diagonally for 4 triangles.
	light	2 squares, 1⅞" x 1⅞"
		Cut once diagonally for 4 triangles.

Stems:
From brown, cut a bias strip, ¾" x 12". Press under ¼" at each raw edge so finished strip is ¼" wide. Place the bias strip diagonally across the corner square for each block as shown in the guide block. Using matching thread, topstitch in place on the background square *before piecing the leaf block*. Stitch them in place, chain fashion, as shown.

Ohio Star

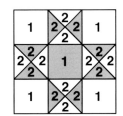

Ohio Star guide block
Make 4
Finished size: 3" x 3"

Cut and piece 4 Ohio Star blocks, with each star made from a different color on a different light fabric. Cutting directions are for 1 block, using pieces #1 and #2.

OHIO STAR BLOCK (ROTARY-CUT)

Piece	Color	Cutting
#1	light	4 squares, 1½" x 1½"
	star color	1 square, 1½" x 1½"
#2	light	2 squares, 2¼" x 2¼"
		Cut twice diagonally for 8 triangles.
	star color	2 squares, 2¼" x 2¼"
		Cut twice diagonally for 8 triangles.

House

Cut and piece 2 House blocks, using pieces #1–#13. Cutting directions are for 1 block only.
Note: The location of the door and window in the lower half of the house has been reversed in the second block for visual variety.

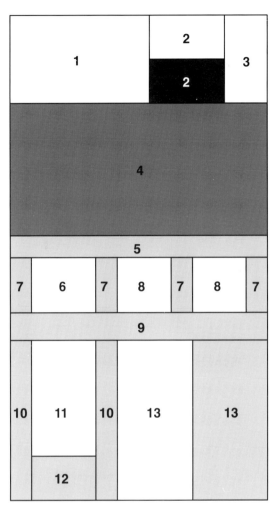

House guide block
Make 2
Finished size: 6" x 11"

HOUSE BLOCK (ROTARY-CUT)

Piece	Color	Cutting
#1	light	1 rectangle, 2½" x 3¾"
#2	light	1 rectangle, 1½" x 2¼"
	black	1 rectangle, 1½" x 2¼"
#3	light	1 rectangle, 1½" x 2½"
#4	roof color	1 rectangle, 3½" x 6½"
#5	house color	1 rectangle, 1" x 6½"
#6	window color	1 rectangle, 1¾" x 2"
#7	house color	4 rectangles, 1" x 1¾"
#8	window color	2 squares, 1¾" x 1¾"
#9	house color	1 rectangle, 1½" x 6½"
#10	house color	2 rectangles, 1" x 3¾"
#11	window color	1 rectangle, 2" x 2¾"
#12	house color	1 rectangle, 1½" x 2"
#13	house color	1 rectangle, 2¼" x 3¾"
	door color	1 rectangle, 2¼" x 3¾"

Roxanne, our very first part-time employee hired seven years ago, and Sue fill orders in our shipping area. Cozy, huh?

Turkey

Cut and piece 3 turkeys, using pieces #1–#7. Cutting directions are for 1 block only.

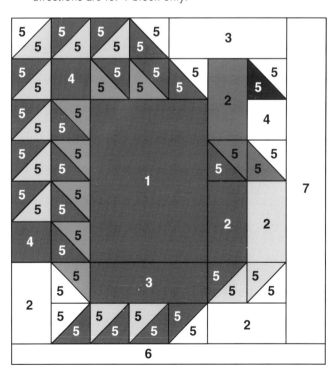

Turkey guide block
Make 3
Finished size: 8" x 8½"

TURKEY BLOCK (ROTARY-CUT)

Piece	Color	Cutting
#1	brown	1 rectangle, 3½" x 4½"
#2	brown	1 rectangle, 1½" x 2½"
	light brown	1 rectangle, 1½" x 2½"
	light	2 rectangles, 1½" x 2½"
	orange	1 rectangle, 1½" x 2½"
#3	light	1 rectangle, 1½" x 3½"
	brown	1 rectangle, 1½" x 3½"
#4	brown	2 squares, 1½" x 1½"
	light	1 square, 1½" x 1½"
#5	brown	11 squares, 1⅞" x 1⅞" Cut once diagonally for 22 triangles. (You will use 21.)
	light brown	1 square, 1⅞" x 1⅞" Cut once diagonally for 2 triangles.
	rust	1 square, 1⅞" x 1⅞" Cut once diagonally for 2 triangles.
	orange	1 square, 1⅞" x 1⅞" Cut once diagonally for 2 triangles.
	black	1 square, 1⅞" x 1⅞" Cut once diagonally for 2 triangles. (You will use 1.)
	red #1	3 squares, 1⅞" x 1⅞" Cut once diagonally for 6 triangles.
	red #2	4 squares, 1⅞" x 1⅞" Cut once diagonally for 8 triangles. (You will use 7.)
	light	5 squares, 1⅞" x 1⅞" Cut once diagonally for 10 triangles. (You will use 9.)
#6	light	1 rectangle, 1" x 8½"
#7	light	1 rectangle, 1½" x 8½"

Log Cabin Apples

Cut and piece 5 Log Cabin apples made from Log Cabin blocks and pieces #1–#3. Refer to the directions for Log Cabin construction on page 8. Cutting directions are for 1 block only.

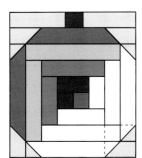

Dotted lines show where connector square is laid. After stitching and folding square over stitching line, triangle forms background corner triangle.

LOG CABIN APPLES (ROTARY-CUT)

Piece	Color	Cutting
#1	light	4 connector squares, 1½" x 1½"
#2	light	2 rectangles, 1" x 2¼"
#3	brown	1 square, 1" x 1"

For the Log Cabin blocks, cut an assortment of red and pink strips, 1" wide. Cut 5 red center squares, 1" x 1". The red strips are color #1 and the pink strips are color #2. These blocks are uneven, requiring 4 red rounds and 3 pink rounds.

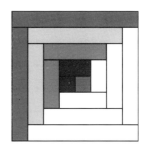

After each Log Cabin block is pieced, position a 1½" connector square of light fabric, right sides together, in each of the 4 corners. Sew diagonally across the 4 squares as shown. See Connector Squares, page 8.

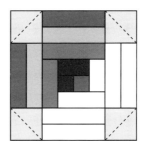

Press each background square to the outside corner of the block, forming a triangle in each corner. Complete the apple block by sewing the stem and background pieces together and then sewing the pieced strip to the top of the apple block.

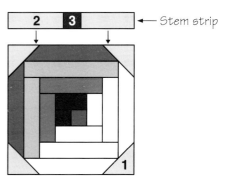

Log Cabin block

3. Spacer Strips and Borders:
   From light fabrics, cut 2 rectangles, 1½" x 3½", for
      the ends of the maple leaf row and 1 rectangle,
      2" x 12½", for the row beneath the houses.
   From purple, cut 3 strips, 1¼" x 44", for the inner border.
   From green, cut 3 strips, 1¾" x 44", for the outer border.
4. Following the quilt diagram below and referring to the
   photo on page 11, sew all the blocks, spacers, and borders together.

5. Using 4 strands of black embroidery floss, embroider the
   turkey feet.

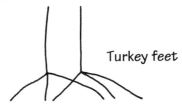

Turkey feet

6. Layer the quilt top with batting and backing. Quilt as desired and bind edges.

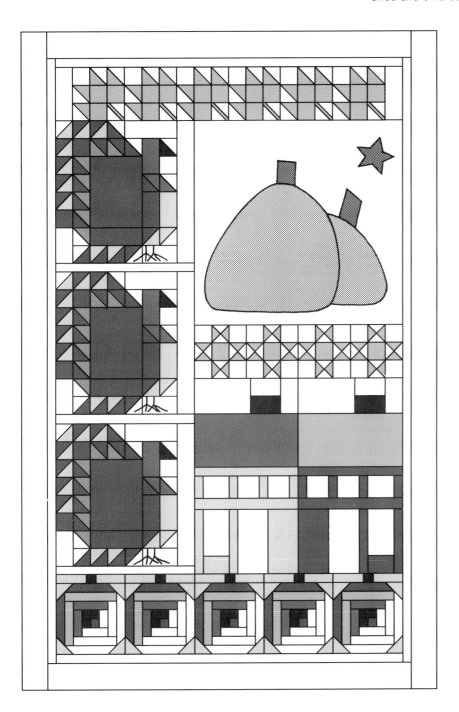

❤ Santa patched his bag but obviously not well enough . . . corn is slowly falling to the ground, but

WINTER

two helpful chickens are quick to lend a hand. This wall quilt with its abundance of scrap fabrics will brighten any home during the holidays or year-round.

Finished Size: 24" x 33½"

Is This Heaven? . . . No, It's Iowa in Winter by Country Threads, 1991, Garner, Iowa, 24" x 33½" . Santa's bag has a hole in it, and corn is falling out for two lucky chickens. Quilted by Gladys Jurgemeyer.

Materials

44"-wide fabric

½ yd. assorted light fabrics
⅓ yd. assorted reds
⅓ yd. assorted teals
¼ yd. assorted greens
⅛ yd. assorted navy blues
⅛ yd. assorted blacks
⅛ yd. assorted browns
⅛ yd. tan checks for beard
Scrap of peach color for face

⅛ yd. red for inner border
¼ yd. teal for outer border
⅛ yd. gold
¾ yd. backing
Batting, binding, and thread
   to finish
6 small yellow buttons
Black embroidery floss

Directions

1. Cut and piece 1 Santa block, using templates 1–28 on
   pages 20–24 and referring to the guide block below.
   Block templates are labeled with the template number,
   block name, and size.

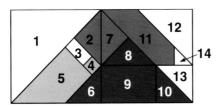

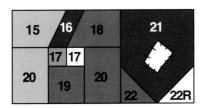

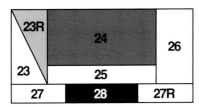

Santa guide block
Make 1
Finished size 10" x 15"

2. Cut and appliqué one Trees with Chickens block, using
   appliqué templates #1–#21 on pullout pattern insert.
      From a light print, cut 1 foundation block, 10½"x15½".
   Appliqué pieces #1–#21, referring to the guide block for
   placement. See page
   7 for appliqué in-
   structions. Using 4
   strands of black em-
   broidery floss, em-
   broider the chicken
   legs and feet.

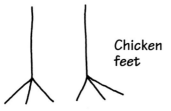

Chicken feet

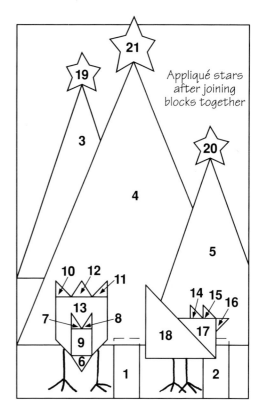

Tree with Chickens guide block
Make 1
Finished size: 10" x 15"

3. Rotary cut the following blocks. Templates are not required. Study each guide block to identify the various
   pattern pieces, which are all labeled by number.

Flying Geese Blocks

Cut and piece 16 flying geese blocks, using pieces #1
and #2. Cutting directions are for 16 blocks.

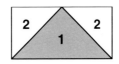

Flying Geese guide block
Make 16
Finished size: 1¼" x 2½"

FLYING GEESE BLOCKS (ROTARY-CUT)

Piece	Color	Cutting
#1	light	4 squares, 3¾" x 3¾" Cut twice diagonally for 16 quarter triangles.
#2	assorted	16 squares, 2⅛" x 2⅛" Cut once diagonally for 32 triangles.

Sew blocks together into strip, referring to the quilt
photo on page 16.

Tree Blocks

Cut and piece 5 tree blocks, using pieces #1–#4. Cutting directions are for 5 blocks.

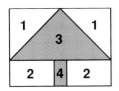

Tree guide block
Make 5
Finished size: 3" x 4"

TREE BLOCKS (ROTARY-CUT)

Piece	Color	Cutting
#1	light	5 squares, 2⅞" x 2⅞" Cut once diagonally for 10 triangles.
#2	light	10 rectangles, 1½" x 2¼"
#3	green	2 squares, 5¼" x 5¼" Cut twice diagonally for 8 triangles. (You will use 5.)
#4	brown	5 rectangles, 1" x 1½"

Sew blocks together into strip, referring to the quilt photo on page 16.

Log Cabin Chicken Blocks

Cut and piece 5 Log Cabin Chicken blocks, using pieces #1–#10 and a Log Cabin block for the center.

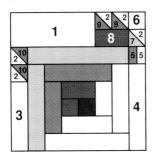

**Log Cabin Chicken
guide block**

Log Cabin Blocks:
Cut an assortment of light and dark strips, 1" wide. Cut 5 center squares, 1" x 1".

Assemble 5 Log Cabin blocks, referring to page 8 for Log Cabin construction. Add 1 extra dark round to the dark side of the block, making it an uneven block with 2 rounds of light and 3 rounds of dark.

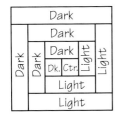

Log Cabin block
Make 5
Finished size: 4" x 4

To turn these 5 Log Cabin blocks into chickens, cut the following pieces and construct the blocks, following the guide block. Cutting directions are for 5 blocks.

CHICKEN BLOCKS (ROTARY-CUT)

Piece	Color	Cutting
#1	light	5 rectangles, 1½" x 3"
#2	light	13 squares, 1⅜" x 1⅜" Cut once diagonally for 26 triangles. (You will use 25.)
#3	light	5 rectangles, 1" x 2½"
#4	light	5 rectangles, 1" x 3"
#5	light	5 rectangles, ¾" x 1"
#6	light	5 squares, 1" x 1"
#7	gold	3 squares, 1⅜" x 1⅜" Cut once diagonally for 6 triangles. (You will use 5.)
#8	red	5 rectangles, 1" x 1½"
#9	red	5 squares, 1⅜" x 1⅜" Cut once diagonally for 10 triangles.
#10	dark	5 squares, 1⅜" x 1⅜" Cut once diagonally for 10 triangles.

4. For checkerboard, cut 1 red strip, 1½" x 44". Cut 1 strip, 1½" x 44", from a light fabric. Sew strips together lengthwise and press seam toward the red fabric. Crosscut into 20 segments, 1½" wide.

Sew 20 segments together into strip.

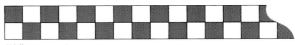

1½" crosscuts

5. For spacers and borders:
   From navy blue, cut 1 spacer strip, 2" x 20½".
   From green, cut 1 spacer strip, 2" x 20½".
   From red, cut 3 border strips, 1¼" x 44".
   From teal, cut 3 border strips, 1¾" x 44".

6. Following the quilt diagram on page 19 and referring to the photo on page 16, sew all blocks and borders together.

7. Layer the quilt top with batting and backing. Quilt as desired and bind edges.

8. Sew yellow buttons on quilt for corn.

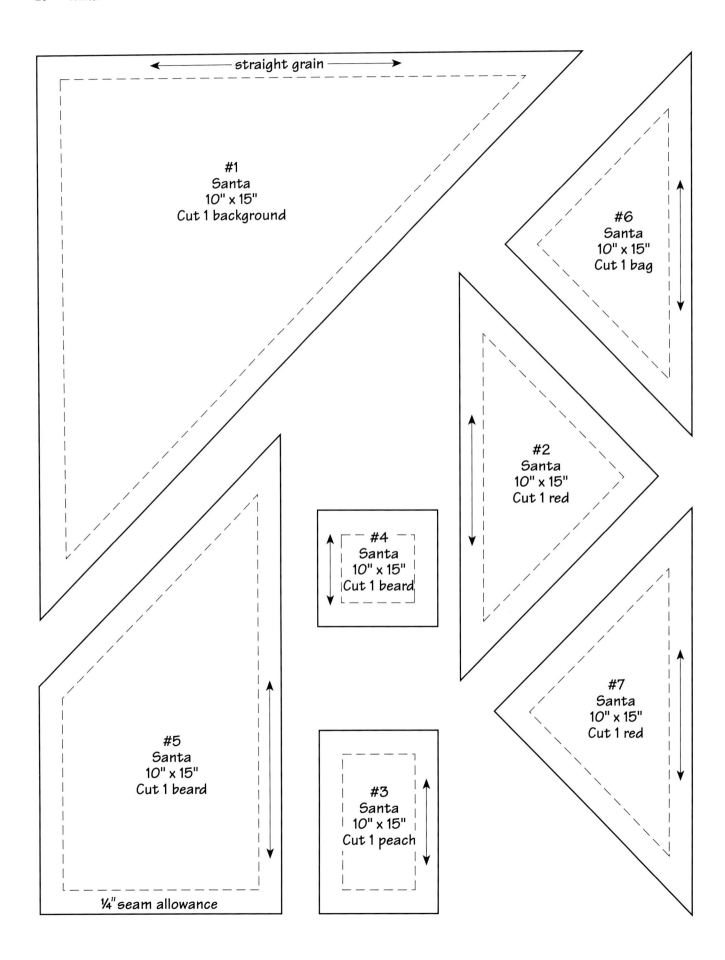

straight grain

#1
Santa
10" x 15"
Cut 1 background

#6
Santa
10" x 15"
Cut 1 bag

#2
Santa
10" x 15"
Cut 1 red

#4
Santa
10" x 15"
Cut 1 beard

#5
Santa
10" x 15"
Cut 1 beard

#3
Santa
10" x 15"
Cut 1 peach

#7
Santa
10" x 15"
Cut 1 red

¼" seam allowance

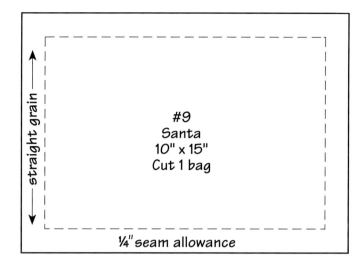

#9
Santa
10" x 15"
Cut 1 bag

straight grain

¼" seam allowance

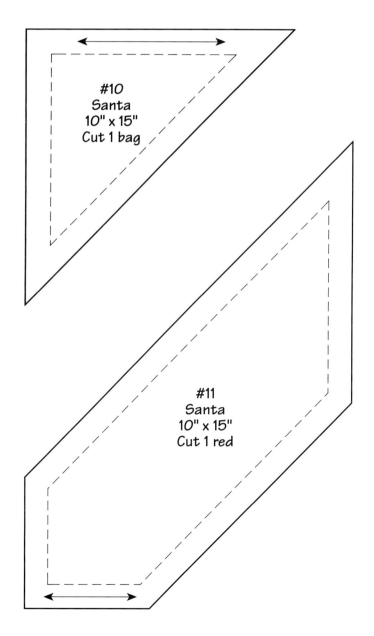

#10
Santa
10" x 15"
Cut 1 bag

#11
Santa
10" x 15"
Cut 1 red

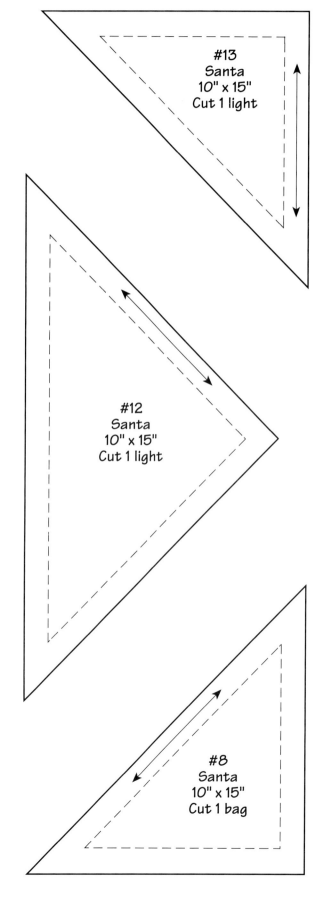

#13
Santa
10" x 15"
Cut 1 light

#12
Santa
10" x 15"
Cut 1 light

#8
Santa
10" x 15"
Cut 1 bag

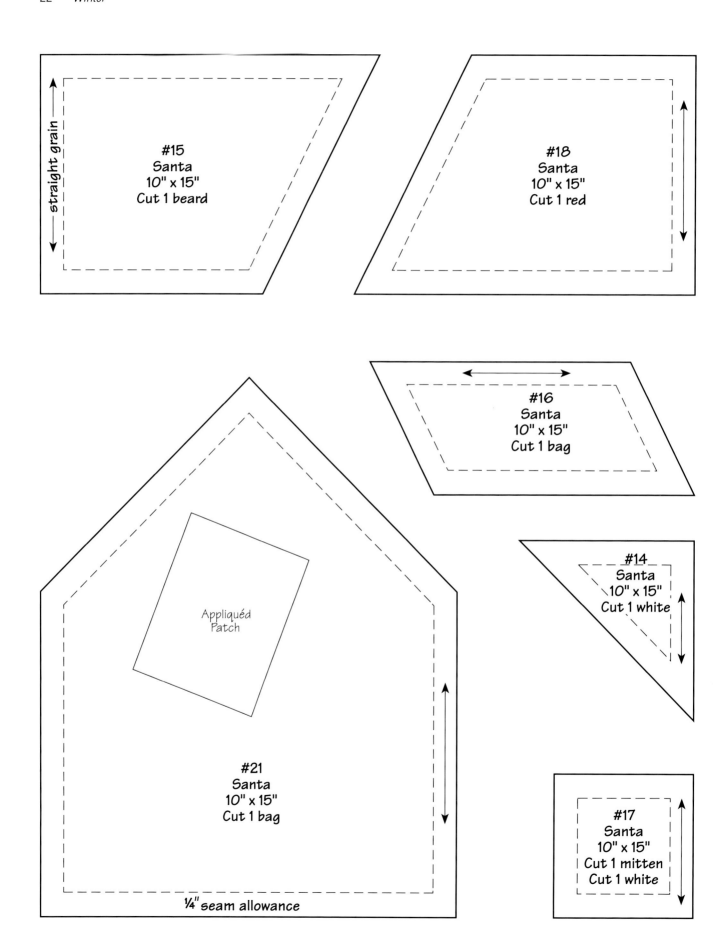

#15
Santa
10" x 15"
Cut 1 beard

straight grain

#18
Santa
10" x 15"
Cut 1 red

#16
Santa
10" x 15"
Cut 1 bag

#14
Santa
10" x 15"
Cut 1 white

Appliquéd
Patch

#21
Santa
10" x 15"
Cut 1 bag

#17
Santa
10" x 15"
Cut 1 mitten
Cut 1 white

¼" seam allowance

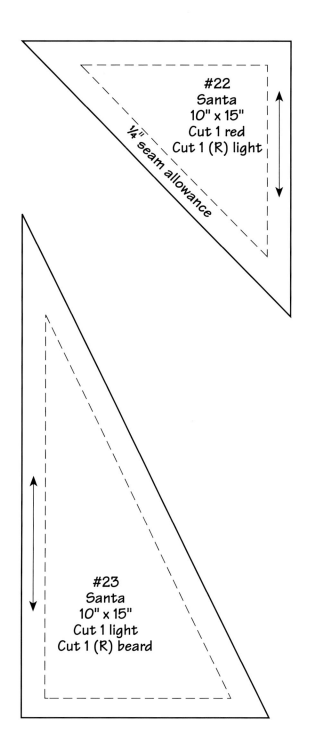

#22
Santa
10" x 15"
Cut 1 red
Cut 1 (R) light

¼" seam allowance

#23
Santa
10" x 15"
Cut 1 light
Cut 1 (R) beard

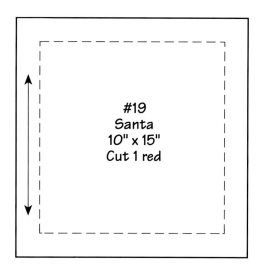

#19
Santa
10" x 15"
Cut 1 red

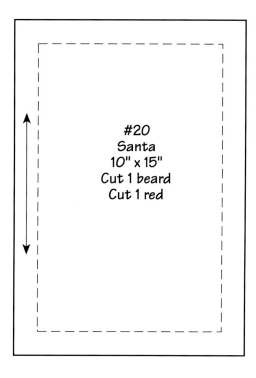

#20
Santa
10" x 15"
Cut 1 beard
Cut 1 red

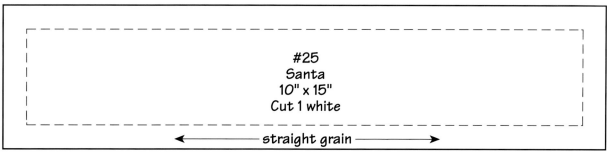

#25
Santa
10" x 15"
Cut 1 white

straight grain

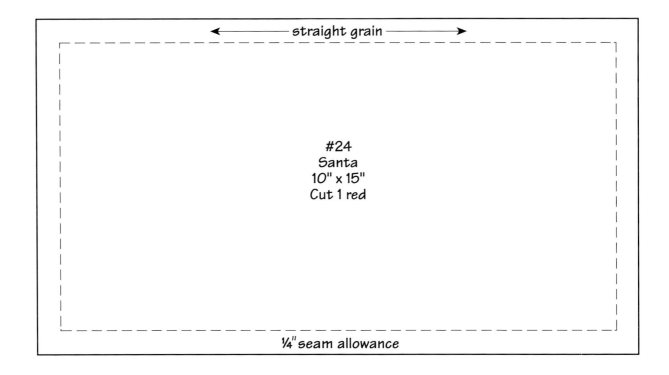

#24
Santa
10" x 15"
Cut 1 red

straight grain

¼" seam allowance

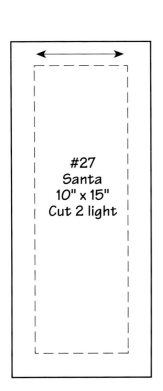

#27
Santa
10" x 15"
Cut 2 light

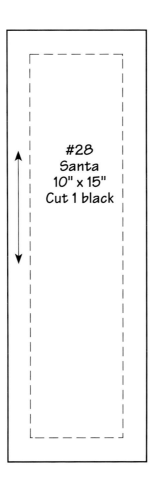

#28
Santa
10" x 15"
Cut 1 black

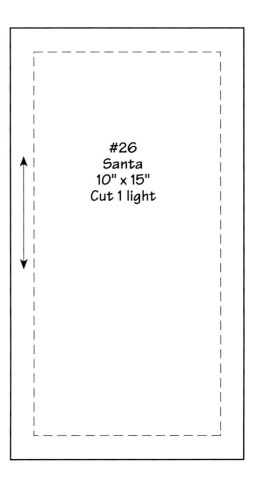

#26
Santa
10" x 15"
Cut 1 light

♥ Tulips are one of the first flowering bulbs that bloom in Iowa after a long, cold winter. And what a welcome sight they are! Festivals are held each spring to celebrate the flowers' arrival . . .

SPRING

one of the largest is held in Pella. This Dutch community boasts of planting bulbs by the thousands each year to the delight of all who visit during tulip festival time.

Celebrate spring where you live with our wall quilt featuring tulips and the ever-present watering can.

Finished Size: 24" x 34"

Is This Heaven? . . . No, It's Iowa in Spring by Country Threads, 1991, Garner, Iowa, 24" x 34". A watering can is combined with spring tulips in this bright wall quilt. Quilted by Gladys Jurgemeyer.

Emma, an eight-year-old, orange tabby cat, rules the quilt shop and "accepts" attention–when she feels like it!

Materials

44"-wide fabric

⅛ yd. gold
¾ yd. tan for foundation
    rectangles
⅓ yd. assorted reds
⅓ yd. assorted blues
¼ yd. assorted greens
½ yd. green solid for bias vine

⅛ yd. red for inner
    border
⅓ yd. blue for outer
    border
¾ yd. backing
Batting, binding, and
    thread to finish

Cutting

From gold, cut:
    8 tulip centers, using appliqué template on pullout pattern
        insert
From tan, cut:
    1 rectangle, 14½" x 18½"
    2 rectangles, 4½" x 20½"
    3 strips, 1½" x 44", for checkerboard
From assorted reds, cut:
    3 strips, 1½" x 44", for checkerboard
    2 strips, 1½" x 18½", for top and bottom sashing
    2 strips, 1½" x 16½", for side sashing
    8 tulips and 3 tulip centers, using appliqué templates on
        pullout pattern insert
From blue, cut:
    1 watering can, using appliqué template on pullout pattern
        insert
From assorted greens, cut:
    all tulip leaves, using the appliqué templates on pullout
        pattern insert
From solid green, cut:
    2 bias strips, ¾" x 20"
    1 bias strip, ¾" x 6"
    1 bias strip, ¾" x 2"
From red for inner border, cut:
    3 strips, 1" x 44"
From blue for outer border, cut:
    4 strips, 2" x 44"

Directions

1. To strip-piece the checkerboard borders, make 2 sets of strips from the red and tan fabrics as shown below. Press all seams toward the red strips. Crosscut each strip set into 20 segments, 1½" wide.

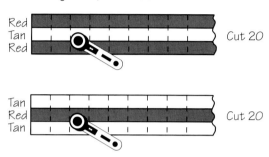

2. Assemble 2 rows of 20 crosscuts each. Press.

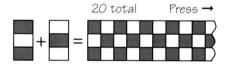

3. Following quilt diagram below and referring to the photo on page 25, sew sashing, blocks, and borders together.

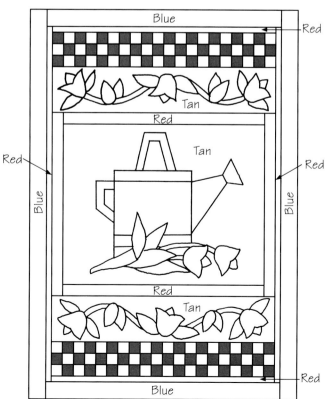

4. Appliqué the watering can and tulips to the large tan foundation rectangle, referring to the quilt plan on page 26 and quilt photo on page 25 for placement. Appliqué the vine, tulips, and leaves to the tan foundation rectangles, referring to the guide blocks for placement. Numbers refer to pattern piece numbers, not order of appliqué. For appliqué instructions, see page 7.

5. Layer the quilt top with batting and backing. Quilt as desired and bind edges.

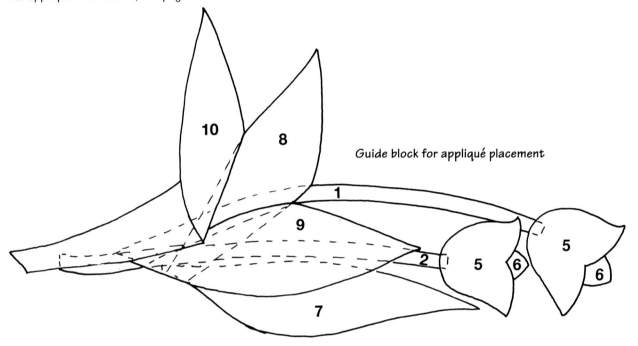

Guide block for appliqué placement

Tulip Vine guide blocks
Make 1 of each

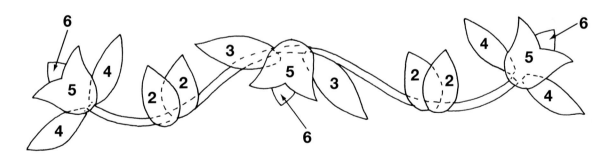

Top appliqué placement

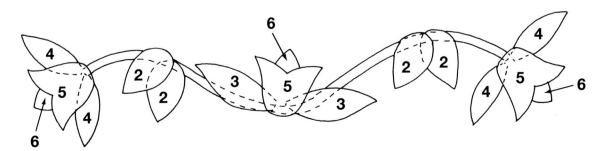

Bottom appliqué placement

♥ Iowa summers bring picnics, Fourth of July celebrations and fireworks, local county fairs, long warm days, and the *garden*.

SUMMER

Innocently planted in April and May, the garden *explodes* with vegetables and flowers all summer long. Apples, tomatoes, carrots, strawberries, green beans, and peas find their way onto the kitchen counter, patiently waiting to be frozen or canned. Long, lazy summer days are few and far between for Iowans. Everyone we know works in the garden all summer long.

Finished Size: 27" x 37"

Is This Heaven? . . . No, It's Iowa in Summer by Country Threads, 1991, Garner, Iowa, 27" x 37". Garden vegetables, along with Fourth of July fireworks and a flag, portray summer in Iowa and the Midwest. Quilted by Gladys Jurgemeyer.

Materials
44"-wide fabric

1 yd. assorted light fabrics
½ yd. assorted reds
⅓ yd. assorted greens
¼ yd. assorted navy blues
¼ yd. assorted purples
¼ yd. assorted browns
⅛ yd. assorted blacks

⅛ yd. gold for inner border
¼ yd. blue for outer border
⅞ yd. for backing
Black embroidery floss
Buttons for peas and flowers
Batting, binding, and thread
   to finish

Directions

1. Cut and piece the following blocks, using the templates on pages 33–36. Block templates are labeled with the template number, block name, size, and number of pieces to cut for 1 block.

Carrot Blocks

Cut and piece 6 blocks, referring to guide block.

Carrot guide block
Make 6
Finished size: 2½" x 5"

Barn and Trees Block

Cut and piece 1 block, referring to guide block.

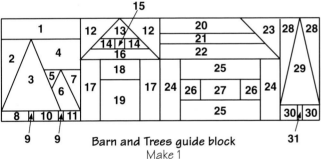

Barn and Trees guide block
Make 1
Finished size: 5" x 16"

2. Cut and appliqué the following blocks, using the templates on pullout pattern insert. See page 7 for appliqué instructions.

Apple Tree

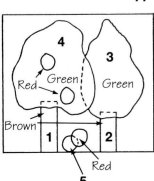

Cut 1 foundation block, 6½" x 7½", from light fabric. Appliqué pieces #1–#5, referring to guide block for positioning.

Apple Tree guide block
Make 1
Finished size: 6" x 7"

Flower Block

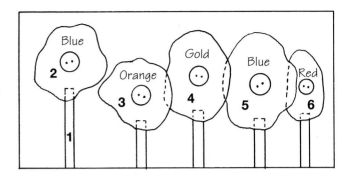

Flower guide block
Make 1
Finished size: 4" x 8"

Cut 1 foundation block, 4½" x 8½", from light fabric. For flower stems, cut a green strip, ¾" x 8". Fold long edges toward center of strip and press so that the finished stem is ¼" wide. Cut 5 stems from the strip.

Appliqué stems and pieces #1–#6 to foundation block, referring to guide block for positioning. Sew buttons on each flower for centers *after* quilting is completed.

Strawberry Blocks

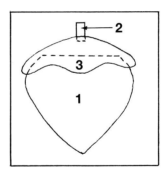

Cut 5 foundation blocks, 3½" x 3½", from light fabrics. Cut and appliqué pieces #1–#3.

Strawberry guide block
Make 5
Finished size: 3" x 3"

Doghouse Block

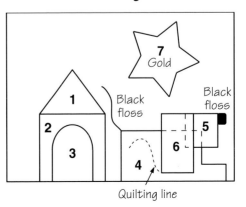

Doghouse guide block
Make 1
Finished size: 5" x 7"

Cut 1 foundation block, 5½" x 7½", from light fabric. Appliqué pieces #1–#7.

3. Rotary cut and piece the following blocks and add appliqués as directed, using the appliqué templates on pullout pattern insert and referring to appliqué instructions on page 7. Study each guide block to identify the various pattern pieces.

Eggplant Block

Cut and piece 5 blocks, using pieces #1–#5. Cutting directions are for 5 blocks.

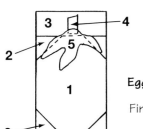

Eggplant guide block
Make 5
Finished size: 3" x 5"

EGGPLANT BLOCK (ROTARY-CUT)

Piece	Color	Cutting
#1	5 different purples	1 rectangle, 3½" x 4½", from each
#2	5 different lights	4 connector squares, 1½" x 1½", from each
#3	5 different lights	1 rectangle, 1½" x 3½", from each
#4	5 different greens	5 stems for appliqué, from each
#5	5 different greens	5 leaves for appliqué, from each

Piece Eggplant block, following piecing diagram and adding connector squares at corners as shown. See Connector Squares, page 8. Appliqué stem and leaves.

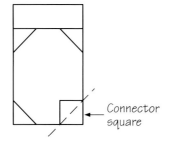

Connector square

Radish Block

Cut and piece 6 blocks, using pieces #1–#4. Cutting directions are for 6 blocks.

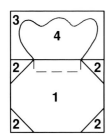

Radish guide block
Make 6
Finished size: 2" x 2½"

RADISH BLOCK (ROTARY-CUT)

Piece	Color	Cutting
#1	6 different reds	1 rectangle, 2" x 2½", from each
#2	6 different lights	4 connector squares, 1" x 1", from each
#3	6 different lights	1 rectangle, 1½" x 2½", from each
#4	6 different greens	radish top for appliqué, from each

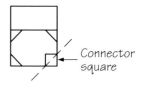

Connector square

4. Rotary cut the following blocks. No templates are required. Study each guide block to identify the pieces, which are all labeled by number. Appliqué radish top.

Pinwheel Star Border

Cut and piece the border containing 11 pinwheel stars, using pieces #1–#4. Cutting directions are for 11 stars.

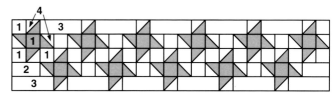

Pinwheel star border guide strip
Make 1
Finished size: 5" x 23"

PINWHEEL STAR BORDER (ROTARY-CUT)

Piece	Color	Cutting
#1	light	23 squares, 1½" x 1½"
	11 different dark star colors	1 square, 1½" x 1½", from each
#2	light	2 rectangles, 1½" x 2½"
#3	light	11 rectangles, 1½" x 3½"
#4	light	22 squares, 1⅞" x 1⅞" Cut once diagonally for 44 triangles.
	11 different dark star colors	2 squares, 1⅞" x 1⅞", from each Cut once diagonally for 44 triangles.

Following the guide strip for positioning, piece the squares, rectangles, and triangle squares together by rows and then sew the 5 rows together.

Flag

Cut and piece 1 flag, using pieces #1, #2, and #7 (star appliqué pattern from Doghouse block).

Flag guide block
Make 1
Finished size: 4" x 23"

FLAG (ROTARY-CUT)

Piece	Color	Cutting
#1	navy blue	1 rectangle, 4½" x 7½"
#2	light	2 strips, 1½" x 16½"
	red	2 strips, 1½" x 16½"
#7	gold	1 star for appliqué

Log Cabin Chicken Blocks

Cut and piece 4 blocks, following the Log Cabin Chicken directions on page 18.

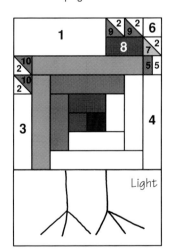

From light fabric, cut 4 rectangles, 2½" x 4½", and stitch one to the bottom of each Log Cabin Chicken block.

Using 3 strands of black embroidery floss, embroider the feet under the chicken body.

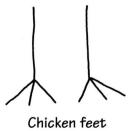

Chicken feet

Onion/Spacer Blocks

Cut and piece 3 onion/spacer blocks, using pieces #1–#4. Cutting directions are for 3 blocks.

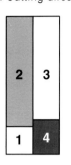

Onion/Spacer guide block
Make 3
Finished size: 2" x 5"

ONION/SPACER BLOCK (ROTARY-CUT)

Piece	Color	Cutting
#1	light	3 squares, 1½" x 1½"
#2	green	3 rectangles, 1½" x 4½"
#3	light	3 rectangles, 1½" x 4¼"
#4	brown	3 rectangles, 1½" x 1¾"

Pea Blocks

Cut and piece 2 blocks, using pieces #1 and #2. Cutting directions are for 2 blocks.

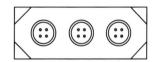

Pea guide block
Make 2
Finished size: 1½" x 4"

PEA BLOCK (ROTARY-CUT)

Piece	Color	Cutting
#1	green	2 rectangles, 2" x 4½"
#2	light	4 connector squares, 1" x 1". See Connector Squares, page 8.

Sew 3 buttons onto each block for "peas in the pod."

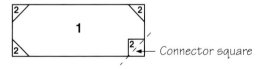

Connector square

5. Rotary cut the borders, cutting across the fabric width (crosswise grain).
   For the inner border, cut 3 strips, 1¼" x 44".
   For the outer border, cut 4 strips, 1¾" x 44".
6. Following the quilt diagram and referring to the quilt photo, sew all blocks and borders together.
7. Layer the quilt top with batting and backing. Quilt as desired and bind edges.

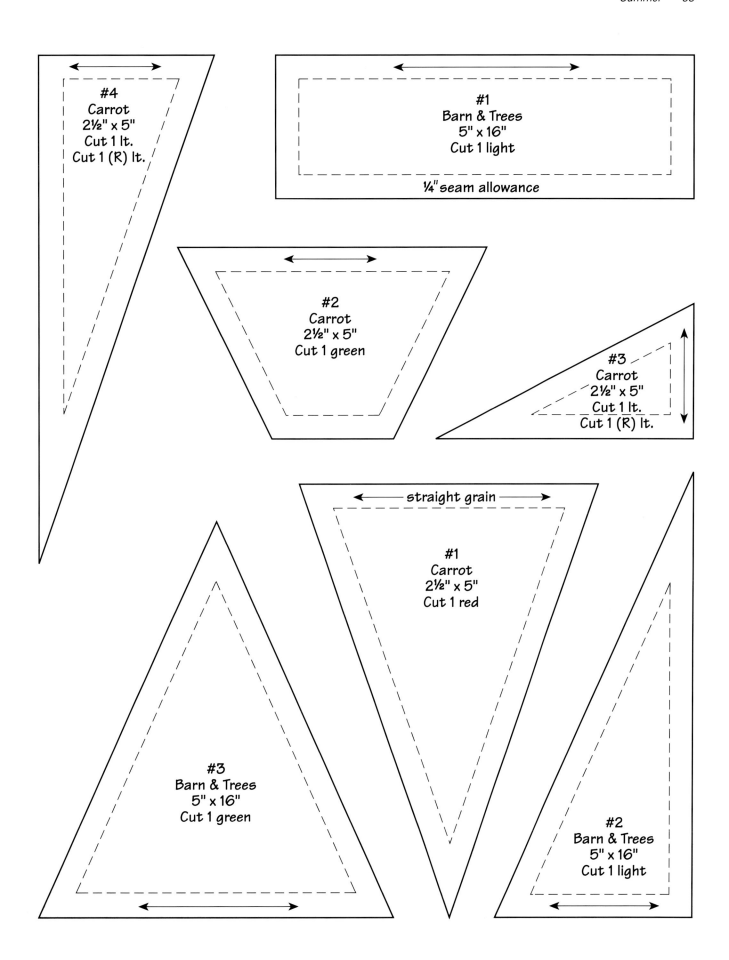

#4
Carrot
2½" x 5"
Cut 1 lt.
Cut 1 (R) lt.

#1
Barn & Trees
5" x 16"
Cut 1 light
¼" seam allowance

#2
Carrot
2½" x 5"
Cut 1 green

#3
Carrot
2½" x 5"
Cut 1 lt.
Cut 1 (R) lt.

straight grain

#1
Carrot
2½" x 5"
Cut 1 red

#3
Barn & Trees
5" x 16"
Cut 1 green

#2
Barn & Trees
5" x 16"
Cut 1 light

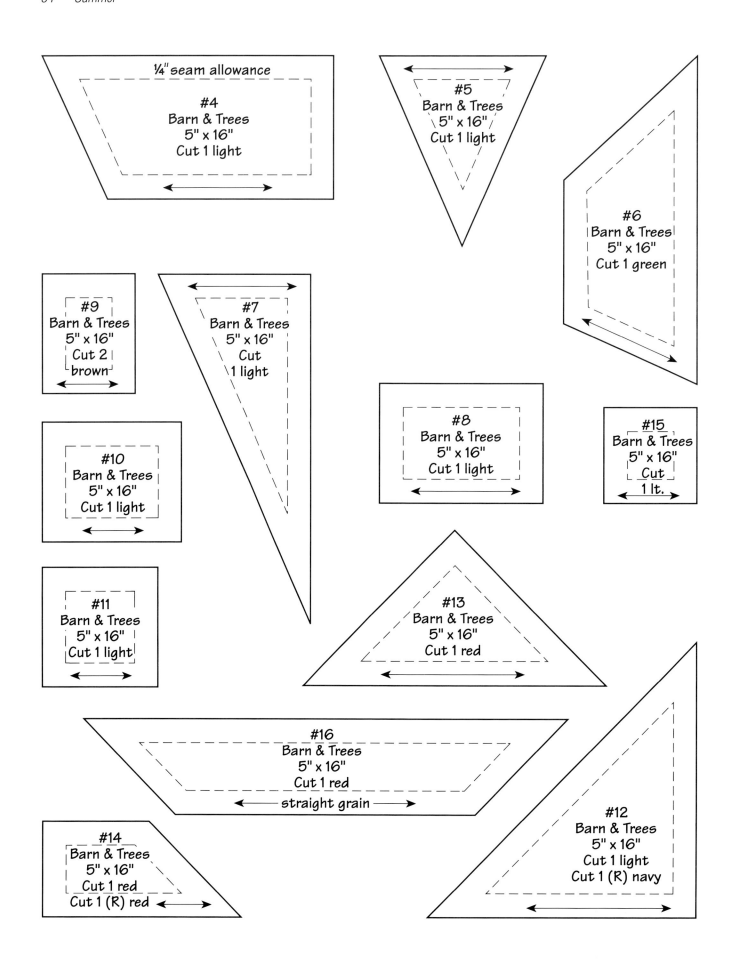

¼" seam allowance

#4
Barn & Trees
5" x 16"
Cut 1 light

#5
Barn & Trees
5" x 16"
Cut 1 light

#6
Barn & Trees
5" x 16"
Cut 1 green

#9
Barn & Trees
5" x 16"
Cut 2
brown

#7
Barn & Trees
5" x 16"
Cut
1 light

#8
Barn & Trees
5" x 16"
Cut 1 light

#15
Barn & Trees
5" x 16"
Cut
1 lt.

#10
Barn & Trees
5" x 16"
Cut 1 light

#11
Barn & Trees
5" x 16"
Cut 1 light

#13
Barn & Trees
5" x 16"
Cut 1 red

#16
Barn & Trees
5" x 16"
Cut 1 red
straight grain

#14
Barn & Trees
5" x 16"
Cut 1 red
Cut 1 (R) red

#12
Barn & Trees
5" x 16"
Cut 1 light
Cut 1 (R) navy

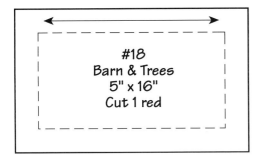

#18
Barn & Trees
5" x 16"
Cut 1 red

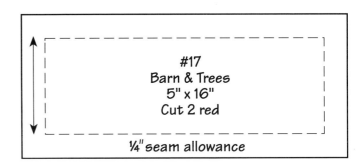

#17
Barn & Trees
5" x 16"
Cut 2 red

¼" seam allowance

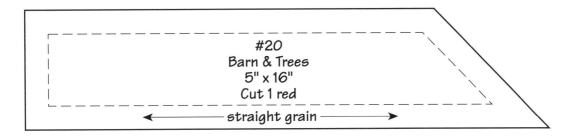

#20
Barn & Trees
5" x 16"
Cut 1 red

straight grain

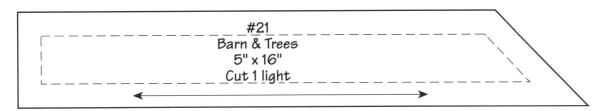

#21
Barn & Trees
5" x 16"
Cut 1 light

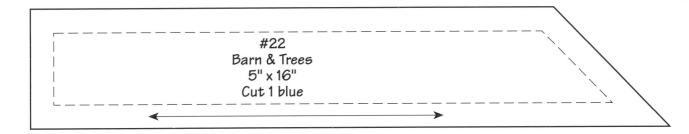

#22
Barn & Trees
5" x 16"
Cut 1 blue

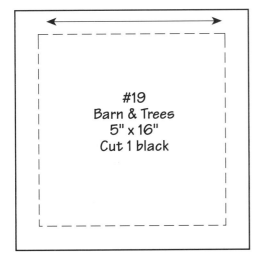

#19
Barn & Trees
5" x 16"
Cut 1 black

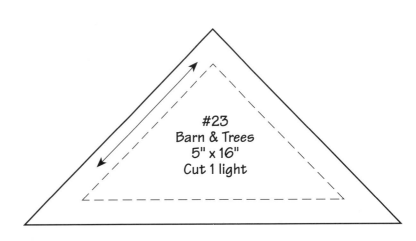

#23
Barn & Trees
5" x 16"
Cut 1 light

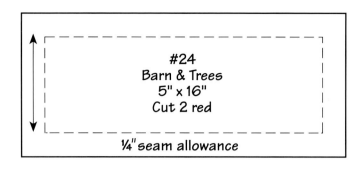

#24
Barn & Trees
5" x 16"
Cut 2 red

¼" seam allowance

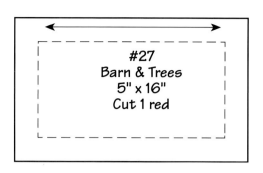

#27
Barn & Trees
5" x 16"
Cut 1 red

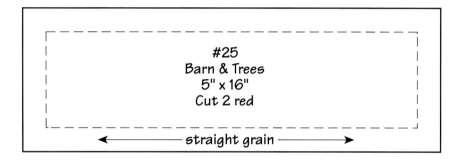

#25
Barn & Trees
5" x 16"
Cut 2 red

straight grain

#26
Barn & Trees
5" x 16"
Cut 2 light

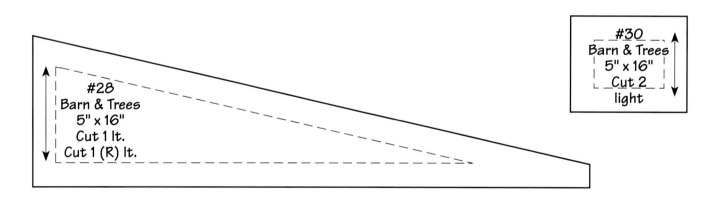

#28
Barn & Trees
5" x 16"
Cut 1 lt.
Cut 1 (R) lt.

#30
Barn & Trees
5" x 16"
Cut 2
light

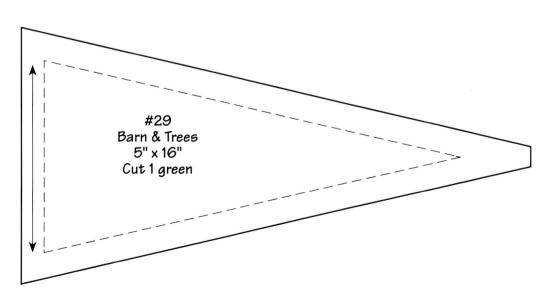

#29
Barn & Trees
5" x 16"
Cut 1 green

#31
Barn & Trees
5" x 16"
Cut 1 brown

ALL ROADS LEAD HOME

❤ If you visit Country Threads, our friendly staff will be happy to point out our overflowing trunk of original quilts from years past. Remaking the quilts in this chapter has opened up a trunkful of memories—memories of drafting patterns, taking photos, and attending the quilt market where each of the patterns was first introduced.

Scrap Basket by Country Threads, 1991, Garner, Iowa, 61" x 61". Red, white, and blue scraps and baskets brighten this patriotic wall quilt. Quilted by Gladys Jurgemeyer.

❤ You've got 'em, we've got 'em, anyone who sews has scraps! Why, we'd even go so far as to assume that if you like quilts, you also like baskets. Our baskets of scraps are the backbone of this

SCRAP BASKET

book and the basis of our philosophy of sewing patchwork. If you like fabric like we do, you'll end up making scrap quilts at some time or another, using all those pieces that are just too good to throw away. If they end up in baskets, boxes, bags, cupboards, closets, and shelves in your home as in ours, here's your chance to use them up!

Finished Size: 61" x 61"

Materials

44"-wide fabric

1½ yds. assorted light fabrics   3½ yds. backing
3 yds. assorted navy blues*   Batting, binding, and
1 yd. assorted reds   thread to finish

*Two navy pieces must be 18" x 18", and two pieces must be 12" x 12".

Cutting

This quilt is completely rotary cut, so no templates are required. Study the guide block to identify the various pattern pieces, which are all labeled by number.

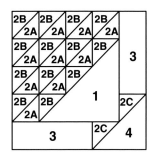

Scrap Basket guide block
Make 13
Finished size: 11¼" x 11¼"

SCRAP BASKET (ROTARY-CUT)

Piece	Color	Cutting
#1	dark	7 squares, 7⅝" x 7⅝" Cut once diagonally for 14 triangles. (You will use 13, for basket bases.)
#2A	assorted darks	65 squares, 3⅛" x 3⅛" Cut once diagonally for 130 triangles.
#2B	assorted lights	85 squares, 3⅛" x 3⅛" Cut once diagonally for 170 triangles. (You will use 169.)
#2C	to match #1 (basket base fabric)	13 squares, 3⅛" x 3⅛" Cut once diagonally for 26 triangles.
#3	assorted lights	26 rectangles, 2¾" x 7¼"
#4	assorted lights	7 squares, 5⅜" x 5⅜" Cut once diagonally for 14 triangles. (You will use 13.)

Setting Triangles:
From navy, cut 2 squares, 18" x 18". Cut twice diagonally for 8 triangles.

Corner Triangles:
From navy, cut 2 squares, 12" x 12". Cut once diagonally for 4 triangles.

Our classroom over the garage is a fun place to meet friends. From left to right are Carol Post, Connie, Carolyn Pope, and Mary.

Note: The setting triangles and corner triangles are overcut and will be trimmed to size after the quilt top is pieced.

Inner and Outer Borders:
Cut a variety of blue strips, 2¾" wide. Cut into random lengths and join all pieces, end to end, to a length of approximately 450".

Middle Border:
From light fabrics, cut 48 squares, 3⅛" x 3⅛". Cut once diagonally for 96 triangles.
From red, cut 48 squares, 3⅛" x 3⅛". Cut once diagonally for 96 triangles.

Directions

1. Referring to the guide block, piece 13 Basket blocks.
2. Following the quilt diagram on page 40 and referring to the quilt photo on page 38, sew blocks and setting triangles together into diagonal rows.
3. Add the corner triangles. Trim corner and setting triangles to within ¼" of the pieced Basket block to allow for ¼" seam allowance.
4. Sew the first pieced border of random rectangles to top and bottom and then to sides of quilt.

5. To make triangle squares for middle border, stitch each red triangle to a light triangle. Press seams toward the red half of the square.

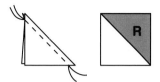

6. Assemble 2 rows, each containing 23 red/light triangle squares for top and bottom. Sew to quilt. Assemble 2 rows, each containing 25 red/light triangle squares for sides. Sew to quilt.
7. Sew the outer border of random blue rectangles to the top and bottom and then to the sides. Press.
8. Layer the quilt top with batting and backing. Quilt as desired and bind edges.

Country Threads Sampler by Country Threads, 1991, Garner, Iowa, 30" x 50".
An assortment of blocks from past Country Threads patterns were used to create
this colorful memory quilt. Quilted by Gladys Jurgemeyer.

❤ This wall quilt is made up of blocks from twelve of our most popular Country Threads patterns, some of which are discontinued. Each block

COUNTRY THREADS SAMPLER

has been made with a scrappy look to give an overall look of old-time charm. Some blocks are made with templates, some blocks are rotary cut, and some are appliquéd. Combining all three techniques in a single quilt is a Country Threads trademark.

Making these blocks was like taking a step back in time to when we started our business. What memories this sampler brought to mind!

Finished Size: 30" x 50"

Materials

44"-wide fabric

1 yd. assorted light fabrics	1 small purchased flag,
½ yd. assorted reds	4½" x 6½" *
¼ yd. red-and-white stripe	⅛ yd. burgundy for 2 inner
¼ yd. assorted teals	divider strips
½ yd. assorted navy blues	¼ yd. red for inner border
¼ yd. assorted greens	⅜ yd. navy blue for outer
⅛ yd. gold	border
⅛ yd. tan	1½ yds. for backing
⅛ yd. black	Batting, binding, and thread
⅛ yd. brown	to finish

* If unavailable, piece a flag, 4½" x 6½", of your own design and trim as directed for Flag and Trees Strip on pages 43–44.

Directions

1. Cut and piece 1 each of the following blocks, using the templates on pages 48–53 and referring to the guide blocks. Block templates are labeled with the template number, block name, size, and the number of pieces to cut for 1 block.

Connie's House

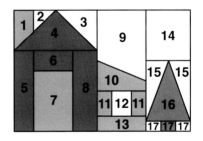

Connie's House
guide block
Make 1
Finished size: 6" x 9"

Andy's House

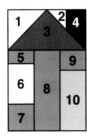

Andy's House guide block
Make 1
Finished size: 4" x 6"

Large Tree

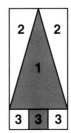

Large Tree guide block
Make 1
Finished size: 3" x 6"

Mary's Farm

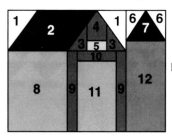

Mary's Farm guide block
Make 1
Finished size: 6" x 8"

2. Cut and piece the following blocks, using the templates on pages 47–48, 53 and referring to the guide blocks.

Basket

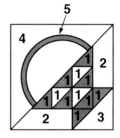

Basket guide block
Make 3
Finished size: 5" x 5"

Bow Tie

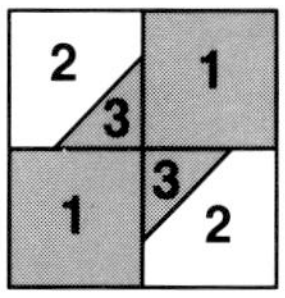

Bowtie guide block
Make 4
Finished size: 3" x 3"

Fish

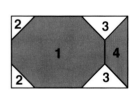

Fish guide block
Make 2
Finished size: 3" x 5"

3. Cut and appliqué the following blocks. See appliqué instructions on page 7.

Ewe Look Mahvelous!

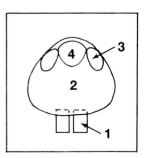

From light fabric, cut 1 foundation block, 5½" x 5½". Appliqué pieces #1–#4, using templates on pullout pattern insert and referring to guide block for positioning.

Ewe Look Mahvelous guide block
Make 1
Finished size: 5" x 5"

Cats!

From light fabric, cut 1 foundation block, 9½" x 9½". Appliqué pieces #1 and #2, using templates on pullout pattern insert and referring to guide block.

Cat guide block
Make 1
Finished size: 9" x 9"

Log Cabin Heart

Log Cabin Heart guide block
Make 1
Finished size: 7" x 8"

a. From light fabric, cut 1 foundation block, 7½" x 8½". Cut an assortment of light and dark strips, 1½" wide. Cut 1 center square, 1½" x 1½".

b. Piece 1 Log Cabin block, referring to Log Cabin construction on page 8.

c. Make and cut out a paper tracing of the heart pattern on pullout pattern insert. Position on Log Cabin block with "dip" of heart at center square. Cut out Log Cabin heart.

d. Cut a bias strip, ¾" x 24", and stitch to raw edge of heart, using a ⅛"-wide seam. Turn bias over edge to wrong side of heart and press. Appliqué to foundation block.

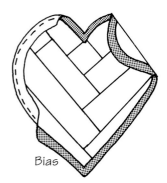

Bias

4. Rotary cut the following blocks. No templates are required. Study each guide block to identify the various pattern pieces, which are all labeled by number.

Treetop Blocks

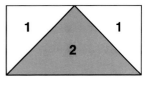 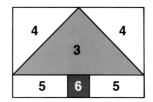

Treetop guide block
Make 12
Finished size: 1" x 2"

Tree guide block
Make 8
Finished size: 2" x 3"

Cut and piece trees and treetops, using pieces #1–#6. Cutting directions are for the 12 treetops and 8 trees required.

TREETOP BORDER BLOCKS (ROTARY-CUT)

Piece	Color	Cutting
#1	light	6 squares, 1⅞" x 1⅞" Cut once diagonally for 12 triangles.
#2	green	3 squares, 3¼" x 3¼" Cut twice diagonally for 12 triangles.
#3	green	2 squares, 4¼" x 4¼" Cut twice diagonally for 8 triangles.
#4	light	8 squares, 2⅜" x 2⅜" Cut once diagonally for 16 triangles.
#5	light	16 rectangles, 1" x 1¾"
#6	brown	8 squares, 1" x 1"

Following the quilt diagram on page 46 and referring to the photo on page 41, sew treetops into a row and trees into a row. Sew rows together.

Flag and Trees Strip

Cut and piece 1 strip, using pieces #1–#7.

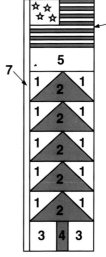

Flag & Trees guide block
Make 1
Finished size: 6" x 21"

FLAG AND TREES STRIP (ROTARY-CUT)

Piece	Color	Cutting
#1	light	5 squares, 3⅝" x 3⅝" Cut once diagonally for 10 triangles.
#2	green	2 squares, 6¾" x 6¾" Cut twice diagonally for 8 triangles. (You will use 5.)
#3	light	2 rectangles, 2¼" x 2¾"
#4	brown	1 rectangle, 1½" x 2¼"
#5	light	1 rectangle, 2¼" x 6"
#6	purchased flag	Trim to measure exactly 4¼" x 6".
#7	black	1 strip, 1" x 21½"

Plaid Basket Block

Cut and piece 1 block, using pieces #1–#4.

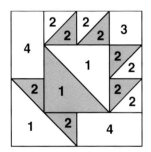

Plaid Basket guide block
Make 1
Finished size: 6" x 6"

PLAID BASKET BLOCK (ROTARY-CUT)

Piece	Color	Cutting
#1	light	1 square, 3⅞" x 3⅞" Cut once diagonally for 2 triangles. (You will use 1.)
	medium	1 square, 3⅞" x 3⅞" Cut once diagonally for 2 triangles. (You will use 1.)
	dark	1 square, 3⅞" x 3⅞" Cut once diagonally for 2 triangles. (You will use 1.)
#2	dark	3 squares, 2⅜" x 2⅜" Cut once diagonally for 6 triangles.
	light	2 squares, 2⅜" x 2⅜" Cut once diagonally for 4 triangles.
#3	light	1 square, 2" x 2"
#4	light	2 rectangles, 2" x 3½"

Delectable Mountains Blocks

Cut and piece 4 blocks, using pieces #1–#4. Cutting directions are for 4 blocks.

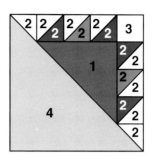

Delectable Mountains guide block
Make 4
Finished size: 5" x 5"

DELECTABLE MOUNTAINS BLOCK (ROTARY-CUT)

Piece	Color	Cutting
#1	medium	2 squares, 3⅞" x 3⅞" Cut once diagonally for 4 triangles.
#2	dark	16 squares, 1⅞" x 1⅞" Cut once diagonally for 32 triangles.
	light	12 squares, 1⅞" x 1⅞" Cut once diagonally for 24 triangles.
#3	light	4 squares, 1½" x 1½"
#4	medium	2 squares, 5⅞" X 5⅞" Cut once diagonally for 4 triangles.

"T" Block

Cut and piece 2 blocks, using pieces #1 and #2. Cutting directions are for 2 blocks.

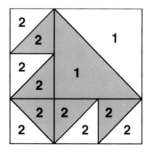

"T" guide block
Make 2
Finished size: 3" x 3"

"T" BLOCK (ROTARY-CUT)

Piece	Color	Cutting
#1	light	1 square, 2⅞" x 2⅞" Cut once diagonally for 2 triangles.
	dark	1 square, 2⅞" x 2⅞" Cut once diagonally for 2 triangles.
#2	light	5 squares, 1⅞" x 1⅞" Cut once diagonally for 10 triangles.
	dark	5 squares, 1⅞" x 1⅞" Cut once diagonally for 10 triangles.

Chicken Block
Cut and piece 1 block, using pieces #1–#10.

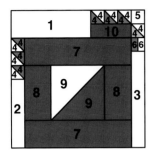

Chicken guide block
Make 1
Finished size: 10" x 10"

CHICKEN BLOCK (ROTARY-CUT)

Piece	Color	Cutting
#1	light	1 rectangle, 2½" x 6½"
#2	light	1 rectangle, 1½" x 5½"
#3	light	1 rectangle, 1½" x 7½"
#4	light	4 squares, 1⅞" x 1⅞"
		Cut once diagonally for 8 triangles. (You will use 7.)
	red	2 squares, 1⅞" x 1⅞"
		Cut once diagonally for 4 triangles. (You will use 3.)
	gold	1 square, 1⅞" x 1⅞"
		Cut once diagonally for 2 triangles. (You will use 1.)
	red stripe	2 squares, 1⅞" X 1⅞"
		Cut once diagonally for 4 triangles. (You will use 3.)
#5	light	1 square, 1½" x 1½"
#6	light	1 rectangle, 1" x 1½"
	red	1 rectangle, 1" x 1½"
#7	chicken color	2 rectangles, 2½" x 8½"
#8	chicken color	2 rectangles, 2½" x 4½"
#9	chicken color	1 square, 4⅞" x 4⅞"
		Cut once diagonally for 2 triangles. (You will use 1.)
	red stripe	1 square, 4⅞" x 4⅞"
		Cut once diagonally for 2 triangles. (You will use 1.)
#10	chicken color	1 rectangle, 1½" x 3½"

Log Cabin Border
Cut and piece 8 Log Cabin blocks.

From red, cut 8 center squares, 1⅛" x 1⅛".

From assorted lights and darks, cut strips 1⅛" wide. Refer to Log Cabin construction on page 8.

Trim completed blocks to measure 3½" x 3½" before sewing all blocks together for the bottom border (3" x 24", finished size).

5. Spacers and Borders:
   From dark-colored fabrics in your assortment, cut:
   1 spacer, 1½" x 15½"
   1 spacer, 1½" x 10½"
   1 spacer, 2½" x 6½".
   From burgundy, cut 2 inner divider strips, 1¼" x 24½".
   From red for inner border, cut 4 strips, 1¼" x 44". Join strips, end to end. From the long strip, cut 2 strips, 1¼" x 24½", for top and bottom borders and 2 strips, 1¼" x 45½", for sides.
   From navy for outer border, cut 4 strips, 3" x 44". Join strips, end to end. From the long strip, cut 2 strips, 3" x 26", for top and bottom borders and 2 strips, 3" x 50½", for sides.

6. Following the quilt diagram on page 46 and referring to the quilt photo on page 41, sew all blocks and borders together.

7. Layer the quilt top with batting and backing. Quilt as desired and bind edges.

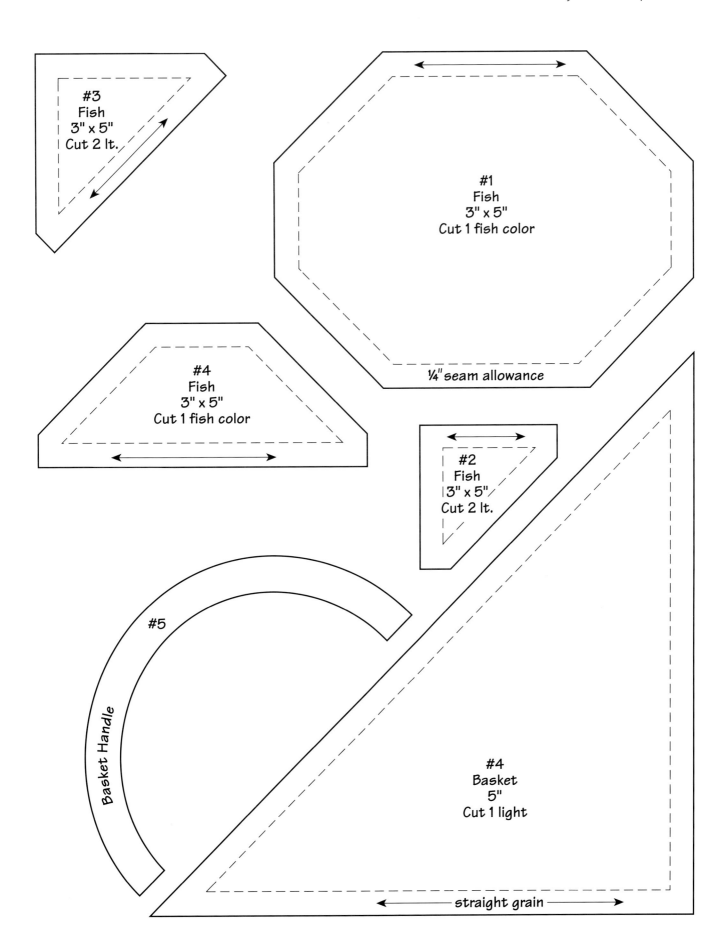

#3
Fish
3" x 5"
Cut 2 lt.

#1
Fish
3" x 5"
Cut 1 fish color

¼" seam allowance

#4
Fish
3" x 5"
Cut 1 fish color

#2
Fish
3" x 5"
Cut 2 lt.

#5

Basket Handle

#4
Basket
5"
Cut 1 light

straight grain

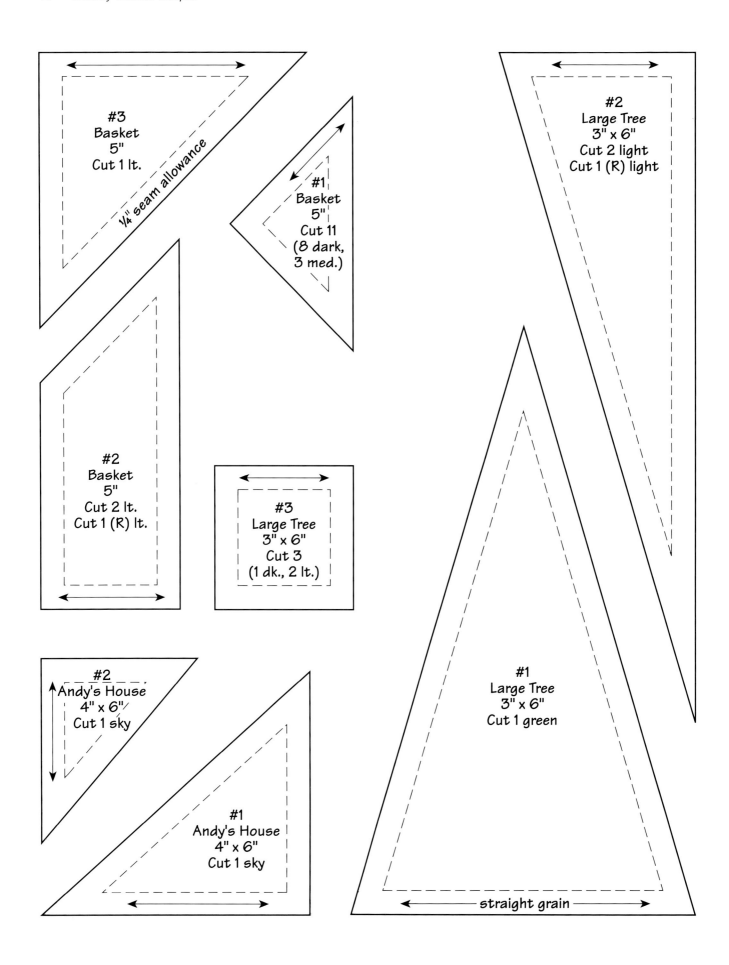

#3
Basket
5"
Cut 1 lt.

¼" seam allowance

#1
Basket
5"
Cut 11
(8 dark,
3 med.)

#2
Large Tree
3" x 6"
Cut 2 light
Cut 1 (R) light

#2
Basket
5"
Cut 2 lt.
Cut 1 (R) lt.

#3
Large Tree
3" x 6"
Cut 3
(1 dk., 2 lt.)

#2
Andy's House
4" x 6"
Cut 1 sky

#1
Andy's House
4" x 6"
Cut 1 sky

#1
Large Tree
3" x 6"
Cut 1 green

straight grain

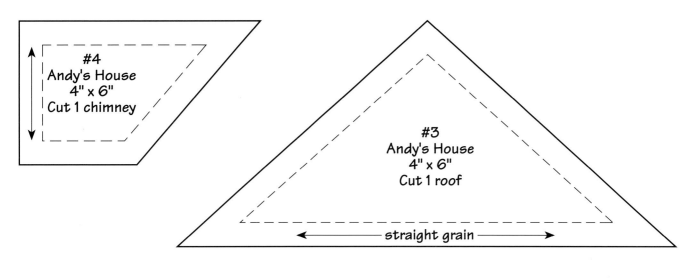

#4
Andy's House
4" x 6"
Cut 1 chimney

#3
Andy's House
4" x 6"
Cut 1 roof

straight grain

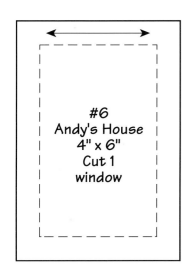

#6
Andy's House
4" x 6"
Cut 1
window

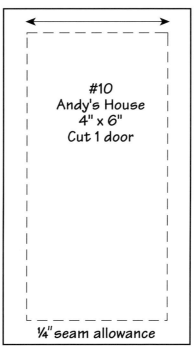

#10
Andy's House
4" x 6"
Cut 1 door

¼" seam allowance

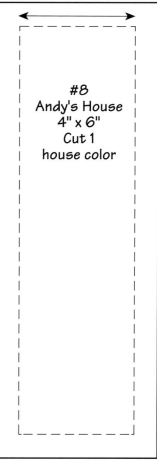

#8
Andy's House
4" x 6"
Cut 1
house color

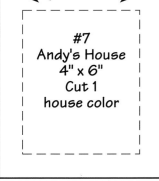

#7
Andy's House
4" x 6"
Cut 1
house color

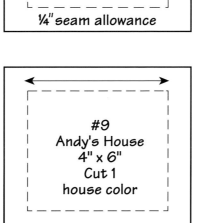

#9
Andy's House
4" x 6"
Cut 1
house color

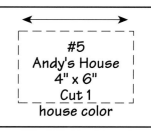

#5
Andy's House
4" x 6"
Cut 1
house color

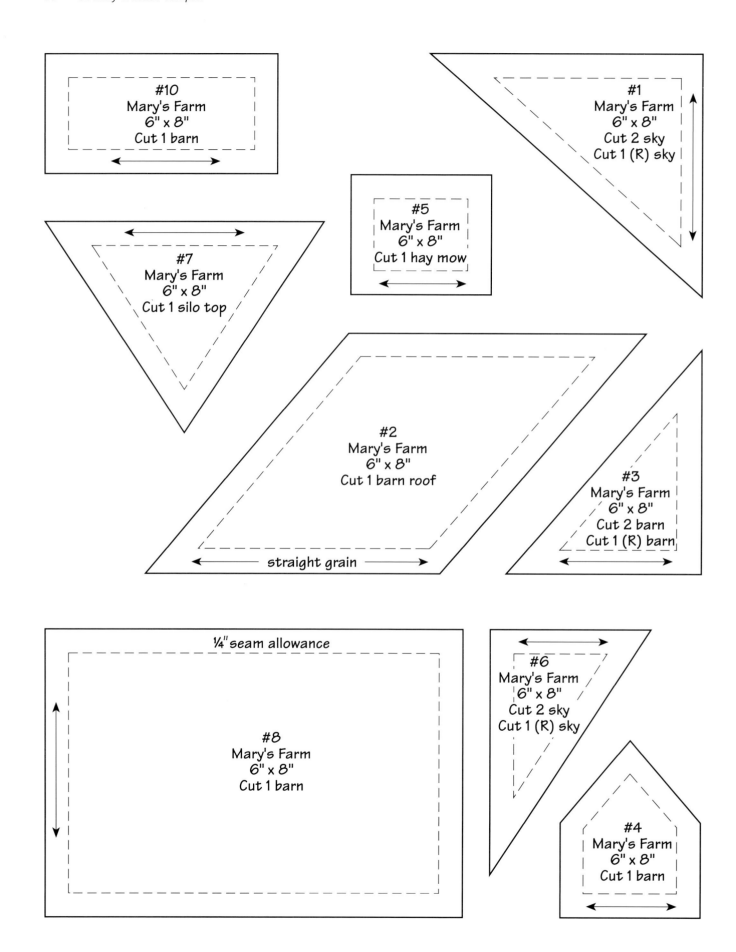

#10
Mary's Farm
6" x 8"
Cut 1 barn

#1
Mary's Farm
6" x 8"
Cut 2 sky
Cut 1 (R) sky

#5
Mary's Farm
6" x 8"
Cut 1 hay mow

#7
Mary's Farm
6" x 8"
Cut 1 silo top

#2
Mary's Farm
6" x 8"
Cut 1 barn roof

straight grain

#3
Mary's Farm
6" x 8"
Cut 2 barn
Cut 1 (R) barn

¼" seam allowance

#8
Mary's Farm
6" x 8"
Cut 1 barn

#6
Mary's Farm
6" x 8"
Cut 2 sky
Cut 1 (R) sky

#4
Mary's Farm
6" x 8"
Cut 1 barn

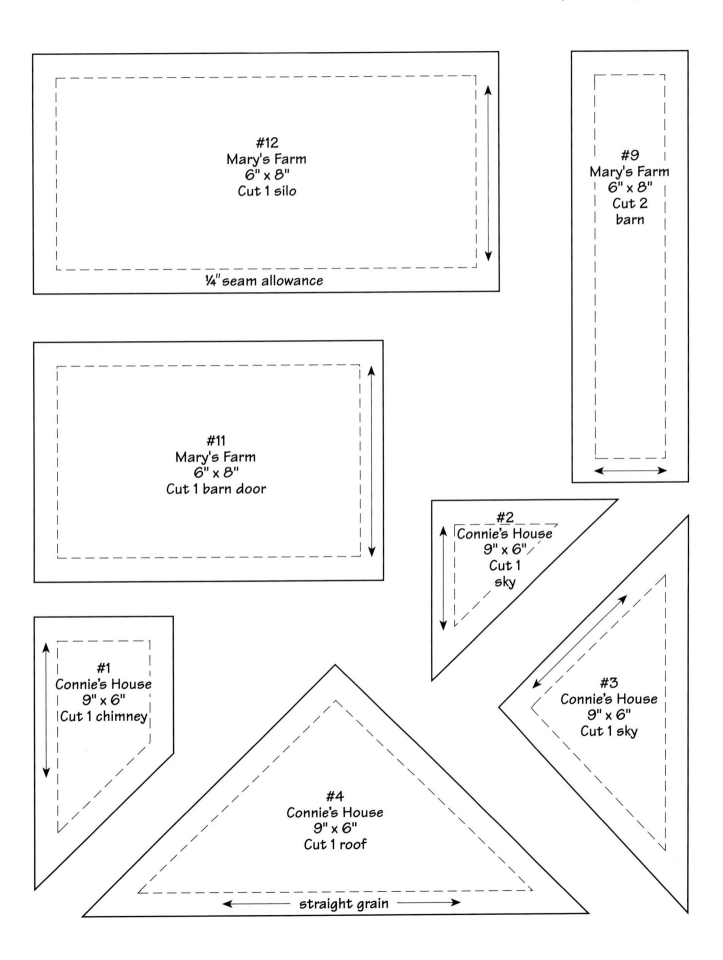

#12
Mary's Farm
6" x 8"
Cut 1 silo

¼" seam allowance

#9
Mary's Farm
6" x 8"
Cut 2
barn

#11
Mary's Farm
6" x 8"
Cut 1 barn door

#2
Connie's House
9" x 6"
Cut 1
sky

#3
Connie's House
9" x 6"
Cut 1 sky

#1
Connie's House
9" x 6"
Cut 1 chimney

#4
Connie's House
9" x 6"
Cut 1 roof

straight grain

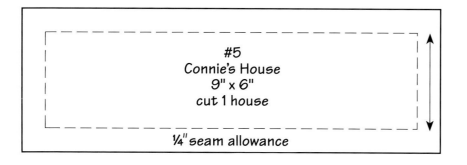

#5
Connie's House
9" x 6"
cut 1 house

¼" seam allowance

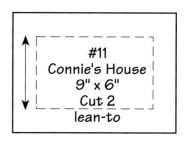

#11
Connie's House
9" x 6"
Cut 2
lean-to

#6
Connie's House
9" x 6"
Cut 1 house

#8
Connie's House
9" x 6"
Cut 1 house

straight grain

#9
Connie's House
9" x 6"
Cut 1 sky

#10
Connie's House
9" x 6"
Cut 1 lean-to

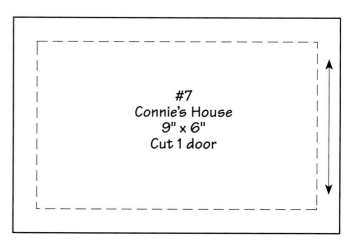

#7
Connie's House
9" x 6"
Cut 1 door

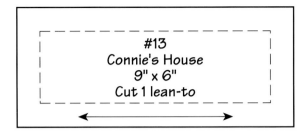

#13
Connie's House
9" x 6"
Cut 1 lean-to

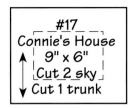

#17
Connie's House
9" x 6"
Cut 2 sky
Cut 1 trunk

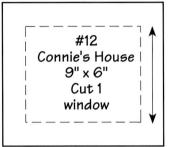

#12
Connie's House
9" x 6"
Cut 1
window

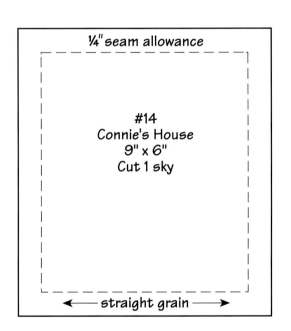

¼" seam allowance

#14
Connie's House
9" x 6"
Cut 1 sky

straight grain

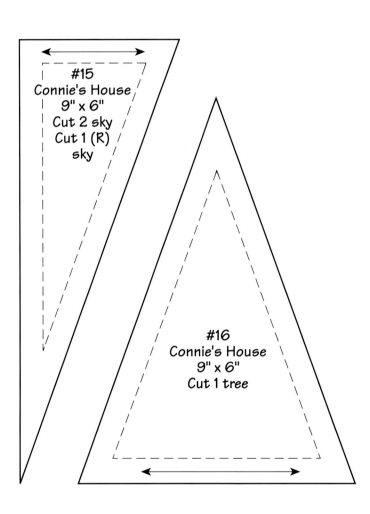

#15
Connie's House
9" x 6"
Cut 2 sky
Cut 1 (R)
sky

#16
Connie's House
9" x 6"
Cut 1 tree

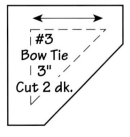

#3
Bow Tie
3"
Cut 2 dk.

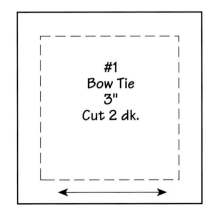

#1
Bow Tie
3"
Cut 2 dk.

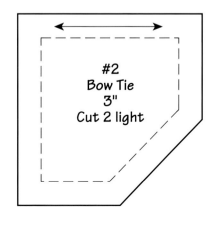

#2
Bow Tie
3"
Cut 2 light

♥ This delightful Christmas quilt takes two popular subjects, houses

OH, MY STARS!

and stars, and combines them

to create a wonderful yuletide treat! Because this quilt is completely rotary cut, you'll have it cut and pieced in no time!

Finished Size: 52" x 68"

Oh, My Stars! by Country Threads, 1991, Garner, Iowa, 52" x 68". Houses and stars create this yuletide quilt. Quilted by Vola Jass.

Materials

44"-wide fabric

¼ yd. each of 6 different checks and homespuns in blue, red, navy, and green for houses

⅛ yd. each of 2 different light-colored fabrics for windows

¼ yd. each of 2 different browns for roofs

⅛ yd. each of 4 different golds for stars

⅛ yd. assorted purples for appliquéd stars

2 yds. red for background, sashing, and borders

3¼ yds. for backing

Batting, binding, and thread to finish

Cutting

House Blocks

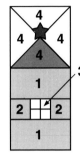

House guide block
Make 24
Finished size: 6" x 14"

HOUSE BLOCK (ROTARY-CUT)

Piece	Color	Cutting
#1	6 different homespuns	8 rectangles, 3½" x 6½", from each
#2	6 different homespuns	8 squares, 2½" x 2½", from each
#3	light	96 squares, 1½" x 1½", for windows
#4	2 different browns	6 squares, 7¼" x 7¼", from each. Cut twice diagonally for 24 roof triangles.

Sashing Stars

From golds, cut 15 squares, 2½" x 2½", and 120 connector squares, 1½" x 1½".

From purples, cut 24 star appliqués.

Background, Sashing, and Borders

From red, cut:

20 rectangles, 2½" x 14½"

18 rectangles, 2½" x 6½"

18 squares, 7¼" x 7¼". Cut twice diagonally for 72 triangles.

6 strips, 3¼" x 44"

Directions

1. Piece 24 house blocks. Using the template below, appliqué purple stars above each rooftop. See appliqué instructions on page 7.

Cut 24 Purple

2. To make the star points for the sashing stars, place 1 gold connector square, 1½" x 1½", right sides together, with one corner of a red sashing rectangle. Sew from corner to corner as shown. Trim away the gold corner but *do not trim off the corner of sashing.* Press gold triangle over seam. Repeat for the other star point. Trim and press.

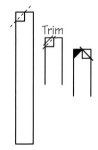

Trim

   Sew the following units, using the remaining connector squares and red sashing strips:

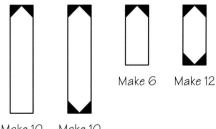

Make 10   Make 10   Make 6   Make 12

3. Following the quilt diagram on page 56 and referring to the quilt photo on page 54, sew the houses, gold squares, and red-and-gold star sashing units together.

4. Sew the 6 border strips together, end to end. Sew borders to the top and bottom of quilt, then to quilt sides.

5. Layer the quilt top with batting and backing. Quilt as desired and bind.

GOING TO BED WITH THE CHICKENS

♥ Each season we hold an all-night class at Country Threads. Students arrive at the farm as the chickens are going to bed at 7:00 p.m. By the time students leave in the morning with their pieced quilt tops completed, the roosters are crowing and the farmyard is bustling. Students bring a dish for a midnight potluck meal and we have show-and-tell of already completed projects. The twelve-hour class is fun and entertaining as well as educational. No one has fallen asleep yet!

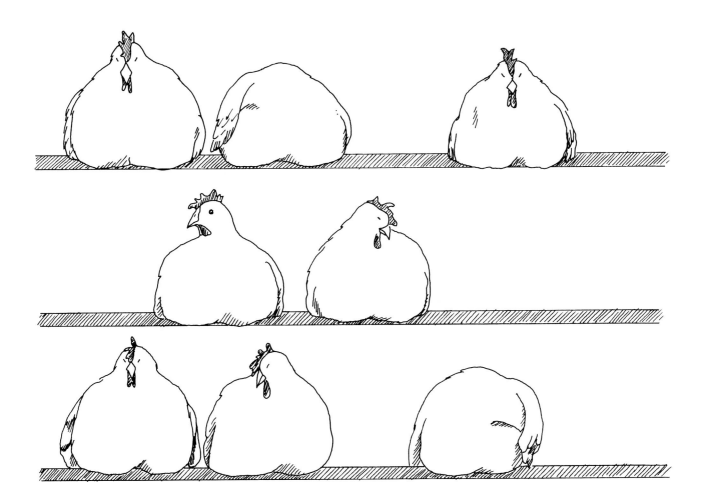

Farmer's Daughter by Country Threads, 1991, Garner, Iowa, 75" x 96".
Brilliant colors and multiple backgrounds are united in this scrap quilt. Quilted by
Elnora M. Paulson.

❤ The subtitle of this quilt comes from firsthand knowledge of being a farmer's daughter. Gathering the eggs was a chore

FARMER'S DAUGHTER
(DO I HAVE TO GATHER THE EGGS AGAIN?)

no one liked, but the farmer's daughter usually got to do it.

This quilt is unique in that all pieces are cut 2¼" wide across the width of the fabric. If you are purchasing ⅛-yard pieces of fabric, they must be cut accurately so that two strips can be cut from each piece. Otherwise, you will have lots of waste and may need to purchase additional fabric. We always cut fabric in our shop with an extra inch or so, in case the piece wasn't cut straight the time before. Our customers appreciate it!

Finished Size: 75" x 96"

Materials
44"-wide fabric

Note: Read all cutting directions *before* purchasing fabric.

4 yds. assorted darks
1¼ yds. assorted bright accents
6 yds. assorted light fabrics
⅓ yd. for inner strip border
⅓ yd. for outer strip border
Batting, binding, and thread to finish

Cutting
All strips are cut across the width of the fabric (crosswise grain).

Star Blocks
From the darks, cut 39 strips, 2¼" wide. Cut each strip into 18 squares, 2¼" x 2¼". Each block requires 13 squares. Set aside the 5 remaining squares from each strip for use in the sashing and/or border, if you wish.

Note: Each block requires one 2¼"-wide strip, so all strips may be cut from different fabrics. If you purchase ⅛-yard pieces, you will get enough squares for 2 blocks from each piece.

From the bright accent colors, cut a total of 156 squares, 2¼" x 2¼", in multiples of 4, for the squares in the center Ninepatch of each block. If cutting them all from the same fabric, cut 9 strips, 2¼" wide, and crosscut for a total of 162 squares.

From light fabrics, cut 39 strips, 2¼" wide. From each strip, cut 4 squares, each 2¼" x 2¼", and 4 rectangles, each 2¼" x 5¾". See note for dark strips, above.

Sashing and Stars
From light fabrics, cut 54 rectangles, 2¼" x 9¼".
From main color darks and bright accents, cut 120 squares, 2¼" x 2¼". Each star requires 5 squares, so cut 24 sets of 5 squares each or use the squares left from the main color strips cut earlier.

Strip Borders
From the inner border fabric, cut 7 strips, 1½" x 44".
From the outer border fabric, cut 7 strips, 1¼" x 44".

Note: The two borders will be a combined finished width of 1¾". If you prefer, cut a single border strip, 2¼" wide, which will finish to 1¾".

Pieced Outer Border
From light fabrics, cut 148 rectangles, 2¼" x 9¼".
From dark fabrics, cut 148 squares, 2¼" x 2¼".

Corner Blocks
From light fabrics, cut 8 rectangles, 2¼" x 9¼".
From dark fabrics, cut 4 squares, 2¼" x 2¼".

Directions
1. Piece 39 star blocks, referring to the guide block and the step-by-step diagrams for adding the connector squares below.

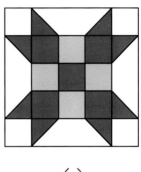

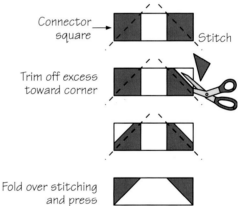

Connector square → ← Stitch

Trim off excess toward corner

Fold over stitching and press

2. Lay out completed blocks with *unsewn* sashing strips and squares as shown below, making sure that each sashing star is made up of squares of the same color.

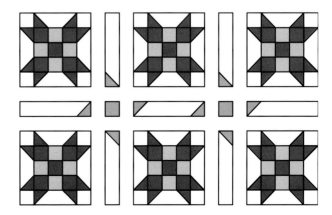

3. Working one row at a time from the quilt layout, make 6 horizontal sashing strips as shown.

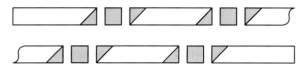

Make 20 vertical sashing strips, piecing 1 sashing rectangle to one connector square as shown.

4. Make 148 border units consisting of 1 rectangle and 1 square, pieced with the square on the right-hand edge of the rectangle as shown.

5. Add 1 border unit and 1 rectangle to 4 star blocks, one for each corner.

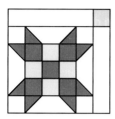

6. Following the quilt diagram below and referring to the quilt photo on page 58, sew all blocks and borders together.
7. Layer the quilt top with batting and backing. Quilt as desired and bind edges.

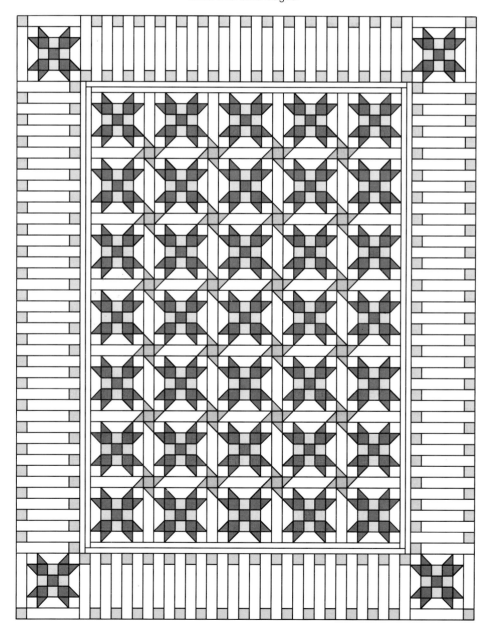

❤ "Grab your partner, all join in!" shouts the caller at a typical barn dance. Traditionally, barn

BARN DANCE

dances were held to initiate newly built barns. What better way to celebrate than to swing your partner and do-si-do around the brand new floor?

With only twenty-four blocks and multiple scrappy borders, this makes for a fast quilt—suitable for either a city or a country bed.

Finished Size: 79" x 85"

Barn Dance by Country Threads, 1991, Garner, Iowa, 79" x 85". Blues and browns mingle in this adaptation of the Delectable Mountains design. Quilted by Elnora M. Paulson.

Materials

44"-wide fabric

4 yds. assorted blues
2 yds. assorted browns
1½ yds. assorted grays
⅔ yd. assorted light fabrics

⅓ yd. for inner border
4⅔ yds. for backing
Batting, binding, and thread
to finish

Cutting

Note: All blocks and borders are rotary cut, so templates are not required. Study the guide block to identify the various pattern pieces, which are all labeled by number.

BARN DANCE BLOCK (ROTARY-CUT)

Piece	Color	Cutting
#1	dark	6 squares, 6⅞" x 6⅞" Cut twice diagonally for 24 triangles.
#2	light	48 squares, 2⅞" x 2⅞" Cut once diagonally for 96 triangles.
	dark	72 squares, 2⅞" x 2⅞" Cut once diagonally for 144 triangles.*
#3	assorted lights	24 squares, 2½" x 2½"
#4	dark	12 squares, 8⅞" x 8⅞" Cut once diagonally for 24 triangles.
#5	assorted darks	4 squares, 14½" x 14½" Cut twice diagonally for 16 setting triangles.**
#6	dark	2 squares, 9" x 9" Cut once diagonally for 4 corner triangles.**
#7	dark	15 spacer squares, 8½" x 8½"

* Triangles may be cut from assorted fabrics or be all the same in each block.

** This is an overcut. (You will trim away excess after piecing quilt top.)

Inner Strip Border: Cut 6 strips, 1½" x 44".

Inner Pieced Border: Cut 1½"-wide strips from a variety of your fabrics.

Middle Pieced Border: Cut 2"-wide strips from a variety of your fabrics.

Outer Pieced Border: Cut an assortment of 6"-wide rectangles of varying lengths from all leftover fabric scraps.

Directions

1. Cut and piece 24 blocks, using pieces #1–#4.

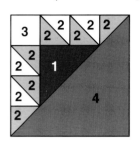

Barn Dance guide block
Make 24
Finished size: 8" x 8"

2. Following the quilt diagram on page 63 and referring to the quilt photo on page 61, sew the pieced blocks, the spacer blocks, and the setting triangles together in diagonal rows, starting at the upper left-hand corner. Add corner triangles last. Trim any uneven outer edges on corner and setting triangles.

3. Sew inner border strips together, end to end. Stitch borders to top and bottom of quilt, then to sides of quilt.

4. Cut strips for inner pieced border into random lengths and sew together, end to end. Stitch to top and bottom of quilt and then to sides of quilt. Repeat with strips for middle pieced border.

5. For the outer pieced border, sew all 6"-wide rectangles together, end to end, and sew to top and bottom of quilt, then to sides of quilt.

6. Layer the quilt top with batting and backing. Quilt as desired and bind edges.

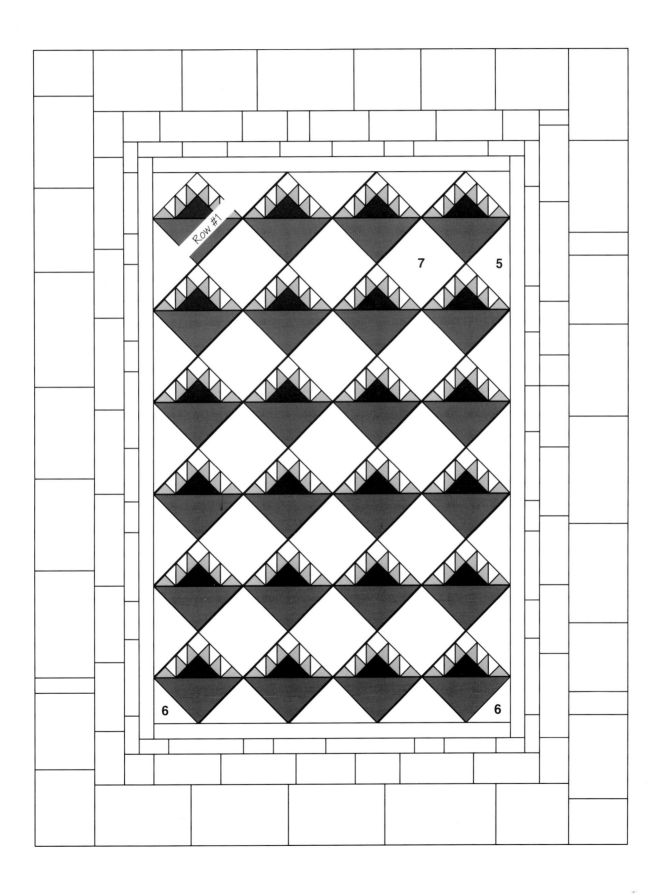

Rabbit Run by Country Threads, 1991, Garner, Iowa, 85" x 108". Overdyed fabrics and a simple checkerboard pattern make this mellow quilt a favorite. Quilted by Marie Thill.

♥ Experimenting with overdyeing fabrics led to this quilt. We love the warm, mellow look overdyeing creates and wanted to use lots of different fabrics together in a

RABBIT RUN

simply designed quilt that would look good in scraps. This quilt, which combines piecing and appliqué, has a pillow tuck built in and three colorful scrappy borders.

Finished Size: 85" x 108"

Materials

44"-wide fabric

6 yds. assorted light fabrics
¾ yd. assorted reds
½ yd. assorted navy blues
¼ yd. assorted rusts
½ yd. assorted golds
¼ yd. assorted browns
¼ yd. assorted light blues

⅛ yd. assorted burgundies
1¾ yd. assorted bright blues
½ yd. for inner border
6½ yds. for backing
Batting, binding, and thread
   to finish

Note: The assorted darks mentioned in the directions include the dark reds, navy blues, rusts, golds, browns, and burgundies.

Directions

1. Checkerboard Blocks:
   Cut and piece 8 Checkerboard blocks, each containing 25 dark squares and 24 light squares.

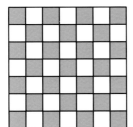

Checkerboard guide block
Make 8
Finished size: 14" x 14"

From assorted dark fabrics, cut 200 squares, 2½" x 2½".
From assorted light fabrics, cut 192 squares, 2½" x 2½".

2. Foundation Blocks for Appliqués:
   Cut and piece 5 foundation blocks, using 3½"-wide rectangles of random lengths. Piece rectangles together and trim each block to 14½" x 18½". Cut and piece 4 additional foundation blocks and trim each to 14½" x 16½".

Note: Refer to quilt photo on page 64 when piecing the foundation blocks. Some are pieced with the strips running horizontally and some with strips running vertically.

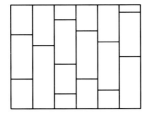

Applique foundation blocks
Make 9 total
Make 5
Cut size: 14½" x 18½"
Finished size: 14" x 18"
Make 4
Cut size: 14½" x 16½"
Finished size: 14" x 16"

3. Appliqués:
   Cut appliqué pieces, using the templates on pullout pattern insert and referring to the quilt photo on page 64 for color placement. Be sure to cut the two rabbits so one is facing left, one facing right. Cut the optional year numer-

als for the watering can and your initials, freehand, if you want them on your quilt.
   Appliqué all pieces to the pieced foundation blocks. See page 7 for appliqué instructions.

4. Spacers:
   From assorted fabrics, cut:
   4 rectangles, 3½" x 6½", for the spacer row between the rabbits.
   17 squares, 2½" x 2½", for spacers at each end of rabbit row and at bottom of spacer row between rabbits.

   In addition, cut an assortment of rectangles, 3½" x 7½", for the spacer rows beneath the rabbits. Sew rectangles together, end to end, and from this strip, cut 3 spacer rows, each 3½" x 46½". Sew the 3 spacer rows together to create the pillow tuck.

5. Inner Border:
   From inner border fabric, cut:
      5 strips, each 2½" x 44", for sides. Sew together, end to end.
      3 strips, each 3" x 44", for top and bottom. Sew together, end to end.

6. Inner Pieced Border:
      This border is sewn to 3 sides only. See quilt diagram on page 66.
   From assorted fabrics, cut 123 squares, 2½" x 2½", and 123 rectangles, 2½" x 8½". Sew a square to the right-hand edge of each rectangle.

   Join these into 2 rows of 49 units each for the side borders and 1 row of 25 units for the bottom border, alternating the location of the squares as shown.

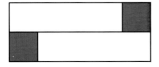

   From assorted fabrics, cut 50 squares, 2½" x 2½", and piece 2 Checkerboard blocks, one for each bottom corner. Stitch one to each of the long side border strips.

Make 2
Finished size: 10" x 10"

7. Middle and Outer Pieced Borders:
   These borders are on the long sides of the quilt only.

From assorted fabrics, cut enough 3½" x 7½" rectangles to piece together for 2 borders on each side of quilt.

8. Following the quilt diagram below and referring to the quilt photo on page 64, sew all blocks and borders together.

9. Layer the quilt top with batting and backing. Quilt as desired and bind edges.

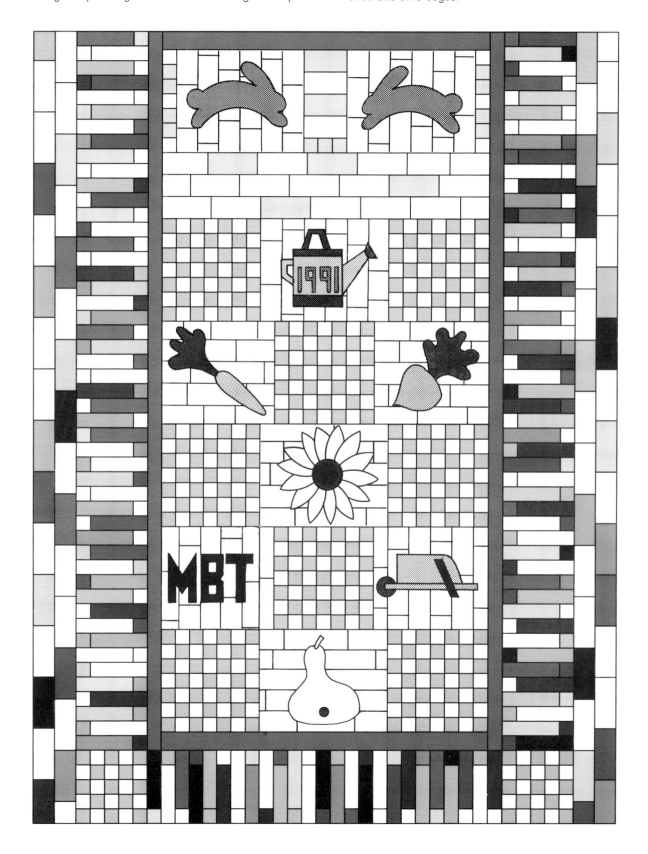

EAST MEETS WEST

❤ Friends, relatives, customers, and acquaintances often ask, "Don't you ever run out of new ideas?" We only run out of time, not ideas! We can't escape them. They come to us at all hours of the day or night—while riding the lawn mower, fixing dinner, doing the laundry, and during every other activity that occupies our time when we're not actually at work! And their country themes always reflect our daily life in rural Iowa.

Noah's Ark—Iowa Style by Country Threads, 1991, Garner, Iowa, 27" x 39½". Pieced farm animals and a barn ark bring this popular Bible story to life. Quilted by Gladys Jurgemeyer.

♥ Old MacNoah had an ark . . . e-i-e-i-o! And on that ark he had two sheep . . . e-i-e-i-o! This

NOAH'S ARK– IOWA STYLE

colorful wall quilt takes the Noah we recognize from Bible stories and puts him smack dab in the middle of Iowa. Country Threads gives you its version of this popular story, complete with a barn and farm animals.

Finished Size: 27" x 39½"

Materials

44"-wide fabric

⅓ yd. navy blue
⅛ yd. gray
½ yd. assorted light fabrics
⅓ yd. assorted reds
¼ yd. assorted greens
¼ yd. assorted blues
⅛ yd. assorted golds
⅛ yd. assorted teals

⅛ yd. assorted blacks
¼ yd. orange for inner
  border
⅓ yd. teal for outer border
1¼ yd. for backing
Black embroidery floss
Batting, binding, and thread
  to finish

Directions

1. Cut and appliqué the following blocks. See page 7 for appliqué instructions.

Ewe Look Mahvelous!

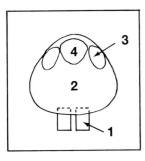

Ewe Look Mahvelous guide block
Make 1
Finished size: 5" x 5"

Cut 2 foundation blocks, 5½" x 5½". Appliqué pieces #1–#4, using the templates on pullout pattern insert and referring to guide block.

2. Rotary cut and piece the following blocks. No templates are required. Study each guide block to identify the various pattern pieces, which are all labeled by number.

Flying Geese

Cut and piece 42 Flying Geese blocks, using pieces #1 and #2. Cutting directions are for 42 blocks.

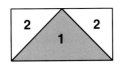

Flying Geese guide block
Make 42
Finished size: 1" x 2"

FLYING GEESE BLOCK (ROTARY-CUT)

Piece	Color	Cutting
#1	assorted darks	11 squares, 3¼" x 3¼" Cut twice diagonally for 44 triangles. (You will use 42.)
#2	assorted lights	42 squares, 1⅞" x 1⅞" Cut once diagonally for 84 triangles.

Sew 21 blocks together into a top border strip (2" x 21", finished size), referring to the quilt photo on page 68. Repeat for bottom border strip.

Log Cabin Chickens

Cut and piece 2 blocks, with one chicken facing right, one facing left. Refer to page 18 for Log Cabin Chicken cutting measurements. Because this block must be 5" x 5", finished, you must add piece #1 to the bottom and piece #2 to each side. See guide block for placement. Cutting directions are for 1 block only.

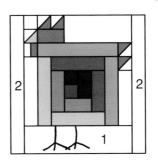

Log Cabin Chicken guide block
Make 2
Finished size: 5" x 5"

LOG CABIN CHICKEN BLOCK (ROTARY-CUT)

Piece	Color	Cutting
#1	light	1 rectangle, 1½" x 4½"
#2	light	2 rectangles, 1" x 5½"

Noah

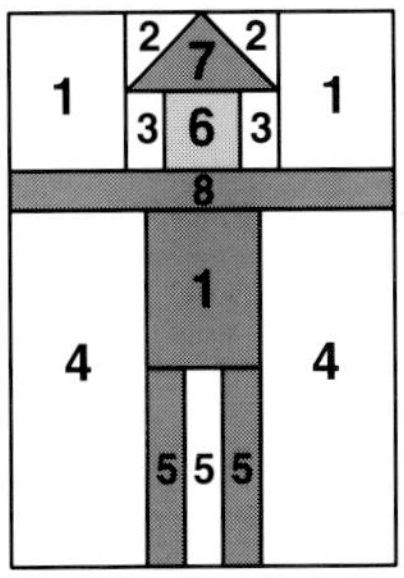

Cut and piece 1 block, using pieces #1–#8.

Noah guide block
Make 1
Finished size: 5" x 7"

NOAH BLOCK (ROTARY-CUT)

Piece	Color	Cutting
#1	light	2 rectangles, 2" x 2½"
	rust	1 rectangle, 2" x 2½"
#2	light	1 square, 1⅞" x 1⅞" Cut once diagonally for 2 triangles.
#3	light	2 rectangles, 1" x 1½"
#4	light	2 rectangles, 2¼" x 5"
#5	light	1 rectangle, 1" x 3"
	black	2 rectangles, 1" x 3"
#6	gold	1 square, 1½" x 1½"
#7	green	1 square, 3¼" x 3¼" Cut twice diagonally for 4 triangles. (You will use 1.)
#8	rust	1 rectangle, 1" x 5½"

Ark

Cut and piece 1 block, using pieces #1 and #2. Refer to Connector Squares, page 8, when adding piece #2 to the bottom corners of piece #1.

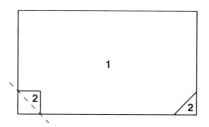

ARK BLOCK (ROTARY-CUT)

Piece	Color	Cutting
#1	navy blue	1 rectangle, 9½" x 16½"
#2	light	2 squares, 2½" x 2½"

3. Rotary cut and piece the following blocks. No templates are required. Each block has a small appliqué detail, which is applied after the block is completely pieced. Study each guide block to identify the various pattern pieces, which are all labeled by number.

Barn

Cut and piece 1 block, using pieces #1–#38. To keep pieces organized for sewing, cut and place each in its correct location in the block on your work surface. Refer to the guide block for position.

Barn guide block
Make 1
Finished size: 14" x 16"

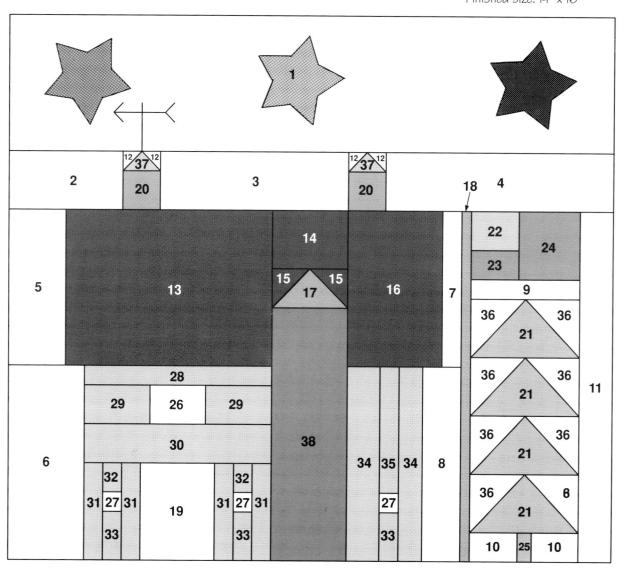

BARN BLOCK (ROTARY-CUT)

Piece	Color	Cutting
#1	light	1 rectangle, 4" x 16½"
#2	light	1 rectangle, 2" x 3½"
#3	light	1 rectangle, 2" x 5½"
#4	light	1 rectangle, 2" x 6½"
#5	light	1 rectangle, 2" x 4½"
#6	light	1 rectangle, 2½" x 5½"
#7	light	1 rectangle, 1" x 4½"
#8	light	1 rectangle, 1½" x 5½"
#9	light	1 rectangle, 1" x 3½"
#10	light	2 rectangles, 1¼" x 1¾"
#11	light	1 rectangle, 1¼" x 9½"
#12	light	2 squares, 1⅜" x 1⅜"
		Cut once diagonally for 4 triangles.
#13	gray	1 rectangle, 4½" x 6"
#14	gray	1 rectangle, 2" x 2½"
#15	gray	1 square, 1⅞" x 1⅞"
		Cut once diagonally for 2 triangles.
#16	gray	1 rectangle, 3" x 4½"
#17	dark red	1 square, 3¼" x 3¼"
		Cut twice diagonally for 4 triangles.
		(You will use 1.)
#18	black	1 rectangle, ¾" x 9½"
#19	black	1 rectangle, 2½" x 3"
#20	green*	2 squares, 1½" x 1½"
#21	green*	1 square, 4¼" x 4¼"
		Cut twice diagonally for 4 triangles.
#22	green*	1 rectangle, 1½" x 1¾"
#23	rust	1 rectangle, 1¼" x 1¾"
#24	rust	1 square, 2¼" x 2¼"
#25	brown	1 rectangle, 1" x 1¼"
#26	light	1 rectangle, 1½" x 2"
#27	light	3 squares, 1" x 1"
#28	red	1 rectangle, 1" x 5½"
#29	red	2 rectangles, 1½" x 2¼"
#30	red	1 rectangle, 1½" x 5½"
#31	red	4 rectangles, 1" x 3"
#32	red	2 rectangles, 1" x 1¼"
#33	red	3 rectangles, 1" x 1¾"
#34	red	2 rectangles, 1¼" x 5½"
#35	red	1 rectangle, 1" x 3¾"
#36	light	4 squares, 2⅜" x 2⅜"
		Cut once diagonally for 8 triangles.
#37	gold	1 square, 2¼" x 2¼"
		Cut twice diagonally for 4 triangles.
		(You will use 2.)
#38	blue	1 rectangle, 2½" x 7"

*A variety of greens was used in our model.

From red, cut 3 stars, using template below, to appliqué above the barn.

With black embroidery floss, embroider a weather vane above the cupola on top of the barn.

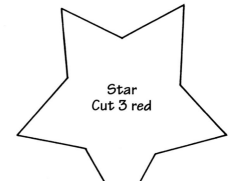

Star
Cut 3 red

Cow #1
Cut and piece 1 block, using pieces #1–#11.

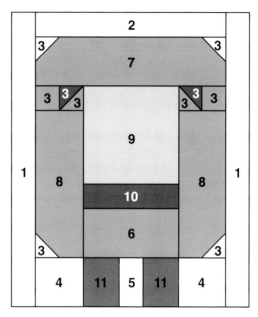

Cow #1 guide block
Make 1
Finished size: 5" x 6"

COW #1 BLOCK (ROTARY-CUT)

Piece	Color	Cutting
#1	light	2 rectangles, 1" x 6½"
#2	light	1 rectangle, 1" x 4½"
#3	light	4 squares, 1" x 1"
	black	2 squares, 1" x 1"
	green	4 squares, 1" x 1"
#4	light	2 squares, 1½" x 1½"
#5	light	1 rectangle, 1" x 1½"
#6	green	1 rectangle, 1½" x 2½"
#7	green	1 rectangle, 1½" x 4½"
#8	green	2 rectangles, 1½" x 3½"
#9	light green	1 square, 2½" x 2½"
#10	black	1 rectangle, 1" x 2½"
#11	black	2 rectangles, 1¼" x 1½"

From gold, cut 1 bell, using template below, to appliqué under cow's head.

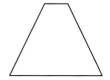

Cow #2
Cut and piece 1 block, using pieces #1–#13.

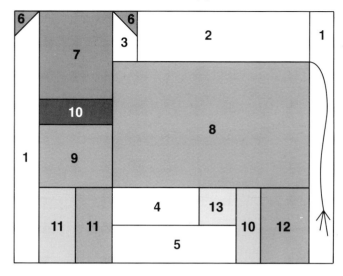

Cow #2 guide block
Make 1
Finished size: 5" x 6½"

COW #2 BLOCK (ROTARY-CUT)

Piece	Color	Cutting
#1	light	2 rectangles, 1" x 5½"
#2	light	1 rectangle, 1½" x 4"
#3	light	1 rectangle, 1" x 1½"
#4	light	1 rectangle, 1¼" x 2¼"
#5	light	1 rectangle, 1¼" x 3"
#6	red	2 squares, 1" x 1"
#7	red	1 rectangle, 2" x 2¼"
#8	teal	1 rectangle, 3" x 4½"
#9	teal	1 rectangle, 1¾" x 2"
#10	teal	1 rectangle, 1" x 2"
	black	1 rectangle, 1" x 2"
#11	teal	1 rectangle, 1¼" x 2"
	black	1 rectangle, 1¼" x 2"
#12	black	1 rectangle, 1½" x 2"
#13	pink	1 square, 1¼" x 1¼"

From gold, cut 1 bell, using template at left, to appliqué under cow's head.

Mailbox

Cut and piece 1 block, using pieces #1–#6.

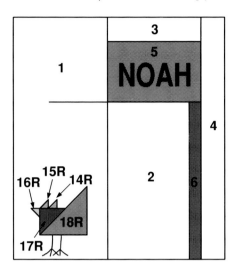

**Mailbox
guide block**
Make 1
Finished size:
4¹/₂" x 5"

MAILBOX BLOCK (ROTARY-CUT)

Piece	Color	Cutting
#1	light	1 rectangle, 2½" x 5½"
#2	light	1 rectangle, 2¼" x 3¾"
#3	light	1 rectangle, 1" x 2½"
#4	light	1 rectangle, 1" x 5½"
#5	red	1 rectangle, 1¾" x 2½"
#6	black	1 rectangle, ¾" x 3¾"

Cut and appliqué the chicken to the pieced Mailbox block, using templates on pullout pattern insert. Cut the body from teal, the head from black, the comb from red, and the beak from gold.

With black floss, embroider "Noah" on the mailbox and a straight line for the open mailbox lid.

4. From light fabric, cut 1 spacer block, 2" x 21½".
From inner border fabric, cut 4 strips, 1¼" x 44".
From outer border fabric, cut 4 strips, 2¾" x 44".

5. Following the quilt diagram at left and referring to the quilt photo on page 68, sew all blocks and borders together.

6. Layer quilt top with batting and backing. Quilt as desired and bind edges.

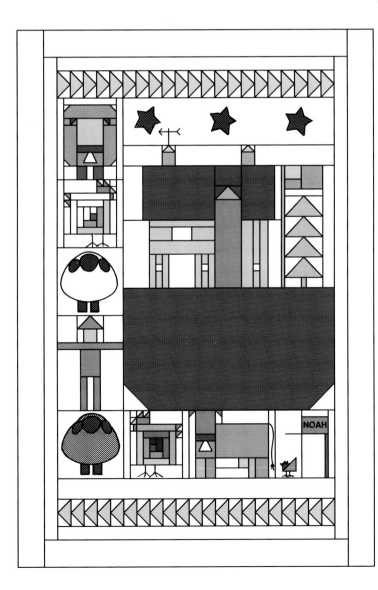

Hometown U.S.A. by Country Threads, 1991, Garner, Iowa, 35" x 49". Traditional Log Cabin blocks and houses form straight furrows. A flag flies overhead. Quilted by Gladys Jurgemeyer.

❤ Every hometown has a flag flying overhead and streets lined with row upon

HOMETOWN U.S.A.

row of houses. In this quilt, traditional Log Cabin blocks sewn up in a multitude of blues and light fabrics form straight "streets" through our hometown. The use of many different fabrics gives a traditional, best-loved quilt pattern a contemporary look.

Finished Size: 35" x 49"

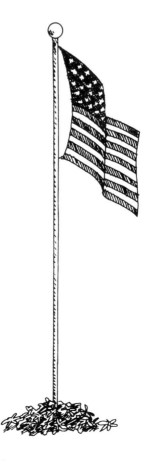

Materials
44"-wide fabric

1 yd. assorted blues
1 yd. assorted light fabrics
¼ yd. assorted reds
⅛ yd. gold

1½ yds. backing
Batting, binding, and thread
  to finish

Directions

1. Log Cabin Blocks:
   Cut and piece 27 Log Cabin blocks, referring to Log Cabin construction on page 8.

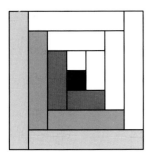

Log Cabin guide block
Make 27
Finished size: 7" x 7"

From red, cut 27 red centers, 1½" x 1½".
From assorted blues and light fabrics, cut a variety of 1½"-wide strips.

2. Flag Blocks:
   Cut and piece the Flag blocks, referring to the guide blocks for color placement.

 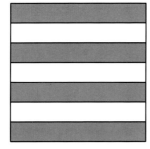

Flag guide blocks
Make 1 of each
Finished size (each): 7" x 7"

From the blue, cut 1 rectangle, 3½" x 7½".
From red, cut 6 strips, 1½" x 7½".
From light fabric, cut 5 strips, 1½" x 7½".
From gold, cut 1 star appliqué, using template at top of page.

**Flag star
Cut 1 gold**

3. House Blocks:
   Cut and piece 6 House blocks, referring to the guide block to identify the various pieces by pattern number. Cutting directions are for 6 blocks.

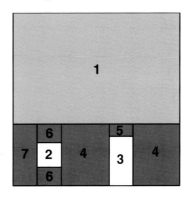

House guide block
Make 6
Finished size: 7" x 7"

HOUSE BLOCK (ROTARY-CUT)

Piece	Color	Cutting
#1	dark	6 rectangles, 5" x 7½", for roofs
#2	light	6 squares, 1½" x 1½", for windows
#3	light	6 rectangles, 1½" x 2½", for doors
#4	6 different darks	12 rectangles (2 per block), 2½" x 3", for house fronts
#5	same 6 darks as above	6 rectangles, 1½" x 1", for house fronts
#6	same 6 darks as above	12 rectangles (2 per block), 1½" x 1¼", for house fronts
#7	same 6 darks as above	6 rectangles, 1½" x 3", for house fronts

4. For chimneys, cut 5 red squares, 2½" x 2½".
   Fold under 1/4" along one edge of each chimney square.
   Press. Fold square in half and, referring to the quilt
   diagram illustration at right, place on lower right edge of
   each Log Cabin block in Row 4. Pin in place with raw
   edges matching along right and bottom edges. These raw
   edges will be caught in the seam. Appliqué folded top
   edge and left-hand edge of chimney to block.

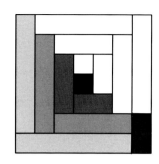

Chimney
placement

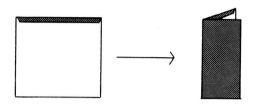

Note: The solitary house in Row 1 has no chimney.

5. Following the quilt diagram and referring to the quilt
   photo on page 74, sew all blocks and borders together.
   Appliqué star on Flag block.
6. Layer the quilt top with batting and backing. Quilt as
   desired and bind edges.

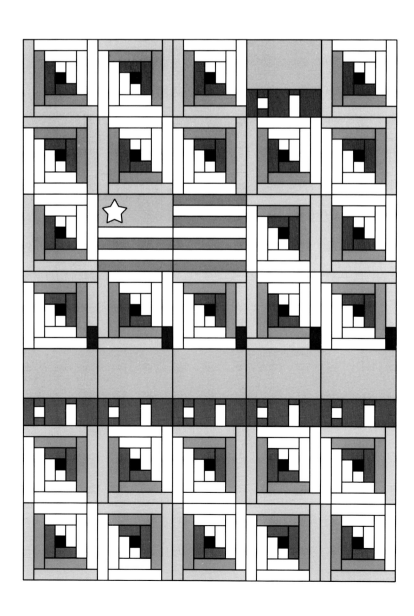

♥ Made from heavy coating wool or scraps of cotton fabric, this Santa stands for peace and joy during the holiday season. Santa becomes a

St. Nick Shepherd

shepherd, with staff in hand, when a woolly lamb stands beside him. A primitive tree with a lopsided star symbolizes the hope of Christmas.

All appliqués are done with buttonhole twist thread and the blanket stitch. The scrap version of the doll is made with a "flip 'n sew" technique on batting. The raw wool beard comes from Country Threads' own four sheep, who all wish you and yours a very MERRY CHRISTMAS! If you would like to order some of our wool, see page 80 for mail-order information.

Finished Size: 7½" x 10"

St. Nick Shepherd by Country Threads, 1991, Garner, Iowa, 7½" x 10". This appliquéd Santa can be sewn up in wool or colorful cotton scraps with primitive blanket-stitch details.

Wool Doll

Materials

¼ yd. heavy wool (red or white)
4" x 4" square of cotton batting for trim
5" x 5" square of green wool for tree
5" x 5" square of brown wool for lamb
Scrap of tan wool for face
Scrap of black wool for staff, sheep head, and ear
Scrap of gold for star
Raw wool for beard
Buttonhole twist for appliqué
2 black buttons
Polyester fiberfill stuffing

Directions

1. Cut 2 pieces of wool, 9" x 12".
2. Make a full-size tracing of the doll shape on heavy paper, using the pattern pieces on pullout pattern insert. Cut out doll shape and trace around it on the *wrong side* of one wool piece.
3. Cut doll front from wool, cutting ¼" outside the drawn line.

Cut ¼" from drawn line

4. Cut out cotton batting trim and tan face, sheep, and staff, or tree and star appliqués, without adding any seam allowances. Position appliqués on the right side of the wool front and stitch in place, using buttonhole twist and the blanket stitch.

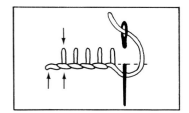

Blanket stitch

5. Place appliquéd doll on remaining wool piece, *right sides together,* and stitch ¼" from raw edges, leaving an open-

ing at the bottom for turning. Trim away excess wool backing next to raw edges of front.

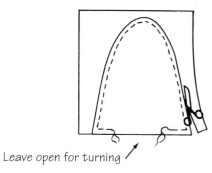

Leave open for turning ↗

6. Turn doll right side out; stuff. Slipstitch opening closed.
7. Glue raw wool beard on face, using glue gun. Glue 2 buttons on doll front.

Flip 'N Sew Doll

Materials

2 pieces batting or fleece, 9" x 12"
1 piece cotton fabric, 9" x 12", for backing
Assorted scraps of cotton fabric
Scrap of tan for face
4" x 4" square of cotton batting for trim
Raw wool for beard
Buttonhole twist thread
Polyester fiberfill stuffing

Directions

1. Cut 2 pieces of batting or fleece, 9" x 12". Cut 1 piece of cotton, 9" x 12", for backing.

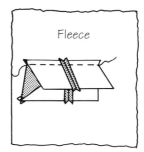

Fleece

2. Position an odd-shaped scrap of cotton fabric approximately in the center of one piece of fleece. Place another cotton scrap on top, right sides together, with raw edges matching, and stitch along one edge through all layers. Press new piece toward fleece. Continue adding scraps in the same manner until the fleece is covered with fabric scraps.

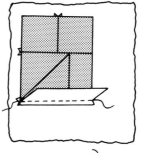

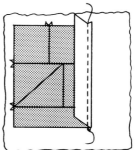

3. Make a full-size tracing of the doll shape on heavy paper, using the pattern pieces on pullout pattern insert. Cut out doll shape and trace around it on the wrong side of the scrap-covered fleece.
4. Cut out doll shape, cutting ¼" outside the drawn line.
5. Cut out cotton batting trim and tan face. Position the appliqués on the right side of the doll front. Stitch in place by hand or machine.
6. Place doll front on backing fabric, right sides together, with remaining fleece on the bottom. Stitch ¼" from raw edges, leaving an opening at the bottom for turning.

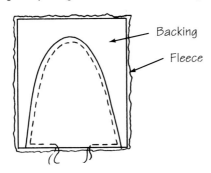

Backing

Fleece

7. Turn doll right side out and stuff. Slipstitch opening closed by hand.
8. Glue raw wool beard on face. If desired, push in bottom corners of doll for a rounded effect and glue or stitch in place.

That Patchwork Place Publications and Products

The Americana Collection by Nancy Southerland-Holmes
    Liberty Eagle
    Old Glory
    Stars and Stripes
    Uncle Sam
Angelsong by Joan Vibert
Angle Antics by Mary Hickey
Appliqué Borders: An Added Grace by Jeana Kimball
Baby Quilts from Grandma by Carolann M. Palmer
Back to Square One by Nancy J. Martin
A Banner Year by Nancy J. Martin
Basket Garden by Mary Hickey
Blockbuster Quilts by Margaret J. Miller
Calendar Quilts by Joan Hanson
Cathedral Window: A Fresh Look by Nancy J. Martin
Copy Art for Quilters by Nancy J. Martin
Country Threads by Connie Tesene and Mary Tendall
Even More by Trudie Hughes
Fantasy Flowers: Pieced Flowers for Quilters
    by Doreen Cronkite Burbank
Feathered Star Sampler by Marsha McCloskey
Fit To Be Tied by Judy Hopkins
Five- and Seven-Patch Blocks & Quilts for the ScrapSaver™
    by Judy Hopkins
Four-Patch Blocks & Quilts for the ScrapSaver™
    by Judy Hopkins
Handmade Quilts by Mimi Dietrich
Happy Endings—Finishing the Edges of Your Quilt
    by Mimi Dietrich
Holiday Happenings by Christal Carter
Home for Christmas by Nancy J. Martin and Sharon Stanley
In the Beginning by Sharon Evans Yenter
Lessons in Machine Piecing by Marsha McCloskey
Little By Little: Quilts in Miniature by Mary Hickey
More Template-Free™ Quiltmaking by Trudie Hughes
My Mother's Quilts: Designs from the Thirties by Sara Nephew
Nifty Ninepatches by Carolann M. Palmer
Nine-Patch Blocks & Quilts for the ScrapSaver™ by Judy Hopkins
Not Just Quilts by Jo Parrott
Ocean Waves by Marsha McCloskey and Nancy J. Martin
One-of-a-Kind Quilts by Judy Hopkins
Pineapple Passion by Nancy Smith and Lynda Milligan
Quilts to Share by Janet Kime
Red and Green: An Appliqué Tradition by Jeana Kimball

Reflections of Baltimore by Jeana Kimball
Rotary Riot: 40 Fast and Fabulous Quilts
    by Judy Hopkins and Nancy J. Martin
Scrap Happy by Sally Schneider
Shortcuts: A Concise Guide to Metric Rotary Cutting
    by Donna Lynn Thomas
Shortcuts: A Concise Guide to Rotary Cutting
    by Donna Lynn Thomas
Small Talk by Donna Lynn Thomas
Stars and Stepping Stones by Marsha McCloskey
Tea Party Time: Romantic Quilts and Tasty Tidbits
    by Nancy J. Martin
Template-Free™ Quiltmaking by Trudie Hughes
Template-Free™ Quilts and Borders by Trudie Hughes
Threads of Time by Nancy J. Martin
Women and Their Quilts by Nancyann Johanson Twelker

Tools
6" Bias Square®
8" Bias Square®
Metric Bias Square®
BiRangle™
Pineapple Rule
Rotary Mate™
Rotary Rule™
ScrapSaver™

Video
Shortcuts to America's
    Best-Loved Quilts

Many titles are available at your local quilt shop. For more information, send $2 for a color catalog to That Patchwork Place, Inc., PO Box 118, Bothell WA 98041-0118.

Mail-Order Information
To receive a bag of wool from Freckles, Munchkin, Mike, or Twinkletoes, send $5 ppd. to: Country Threads, RR2, Garner, Iowa 50438.

We will include our latest catalog free of charge with your order. To receive a Country Threads catalog only, send $1.50 to the above address.